THE SCHILLEBEECKX CASE

THE SCHILLEBEECKX CASE

Official Exchange of letters and documents in
the investigation of Fr. Edward Schillebeeckx, O.P.
by the Sacred Congregation for the
Doctrine of the Faith.
1976 — 1980

Edited, with Introduction and Notes, by
TED SCHOOF, O.P.

Originally published under the Auspices of the
Tijdschrift voor Theologie

Translated by
MATTHEW J. O'CONNELL

PAULIST PRESS
New York/Ramsey

Originally published as *De Zaak Schillebeeckx* by Uitgeverij H. Nelissen B.V. in Holland © 1980.

English translation © 1984 by The Missionary Society of St. Paul the Apostle in the State of New York.

Library of Congress
Catalog Card Number: 83-62389

ISBN: 0-8091-2607-9

Published by Paulist Press
545 Island Road, Ramsey, N.J. 07446

Printed and bound in the
United States of America

Contents

Abbreviations vi

INTRODUCTION 1

CONGREGATION OF FAITH TO SCHILLEBEECKX
First Questions, October 20, 1976 13
  Introduction 15
  THE QUESTIONNAIRE 18
  A Few Words in Conclusion 39

SCHILLEBEECKX TO CONGREGATION OF FAITH
April 13, 1977 41
  Introduction 43
  THE RESPONSE 46

CONGREGATION OF FAITH TO SCHILLEBEECKX
July 6, 1978 69
  Introduction 71
  EVALUATION OF ANSWERS 75

THE CONVERSATION IN ROME
December 13–15, 1979 109
  Introduction 111
  THE CONVERSATION 116

CONCLUSIONS
November 20, 1980 135
  Introduction 137
  THE LETTER 141
  Attached Note 145

EPILOGUE 151

Abbreviations

AAS   *Acta Apostolicae Sedis*

DS   Henry Denzinger and Adolf Schönmetzer, *Enchiridion Symbolorum*, 32nd ed. Freiburg, 1963

TDNT   Gerhard Kittel (ed.), *Theological Dictionary of the New Testament*

INTRODUCTION

Like most Forewords this is also an Afterword. In fact, the book in its entirety may be regarded as an Afterword, for its purpose is to make available, after the event, the various documents of what should be called nothing less than "the Schillebeeckx case": an "investigation" (the Congregation for the Doctrine of the Faith insists that there is no question of a trial, although such an "investigation" may be followed by a condemnation[1]) into the orthodoxy of *Jezus: Het verhaal van een levende* (ET: *Jesus: An Experiment in Christology*) by Edward Schillebeeckx, a scholarly study of some 600 pages in Dutch (and 750 in English) that nevertheless became a best seller.

The "Schillebeeckx case" was an emotionally charged episode in relations between "Rome" and a prominent representative of Catholic theology, and many persons, especially in the Churches of the Netherlands, felt deeply involved in it. The present book, then, is an Afterword on this affair. In preparing this edition I have had to spend quite some time in an intensive study of the "documents." It has been an intriguing but also, and above all, a depressing experience. This is due chiefly to the fact that, behind the often formal and abstract sentences, unexpressed thoughts and feelings of many kinds may be conjectured. In addition, the texts which I had to use were heavily "annotated" by the pen of the accused as he prepared his defense. As a result, something of the unnerving character of the "trial" left its mark on the paper and could readily be felt. The involvement of the participants—the censors, the accused, *and* the reader—is at times very intense. The ultimate issue is, after all, what we are to regard as the supreme value and content of the faith—although this is certainly not always the only thing the papers are concerned with; but a psychologist could speak better to this point than a theologian can.

Furthermore, the chief impression left by a careful reading of the documents is that there is obviously an almost insuperable barrier to mutual understanding on the part of the two sides or, more accurately, on the part of "Rome" in regard to Schillebeeckx. For Schillebeeckx is still quite familiar with the traditional theological language of his opponents, since he was educated in it and himself had to use it in the past. The theologians of the Congregation, on the contrary, have, as it were, hardly any antennas capable of receiving the kind of language Schillebeeckx uses. They translate what he says into traditional Scholastic expressions and then force him to play their language-game. The barrier is, of course, not solely a matter of language; a whole vital attitude also plays a part. Schillebeeckx himself has had some enlightening things to say about this in—among other writings—the controverted book itself.[2] This can be pointed out more concretely in the individual documents.

Why should the dossier of what has not unjustly been called a "dialogue of the deaf" (Hebblethwaite) be published after the event?

First of all, to give a public accounting. When it gradually became clear in the fall of 1979 that rumors about a new action against Schillebeeckx (an "investigation" in 1968 had already been dropped due to protests) were proving to be correct, one of the objections most often heard in the swiftly mounting stream of protests was to the secrecy of the procedure. It turned out that about three years earlier Schillebeeckx had already received an extensive questionnaire and had subsequently returned a detailed answer. As a result, an even lengthier document with further questions had reached him, along with an invitation to a conversation in Rome with three unnamed representatives of the Congregation—men whom he was asked to assume, on their own authority, to be "good theologians." At a still earlier time, therefore—in keeping with the current regulations of the Congregation—some theologians must have studied Schillebeeckx' book in search of "erroneous or dangerous opinions," while another had emphasized the good points in the book—but without the author being aware of any such investigation. A report of these activities had subsequently convinced the cardinals of the Congregation that the author must be asked for clarification, and the Pope had then confirmed this decision. At this point, while Rome reached the end of the "investigatory procedure" that might lead to a condemnation, now the accused himself at last was informed of the situation. But he was given no access to the material which served for the indictment nor even to the names of the investigators.

This course of events elicited a great deal of protest. Society today will no longer suffer anyone in authority to deal with someone's convictions in such a way that cannot be checked. There is an immediate suspicion that things are going on which cannot stand the light of day. Even if people are far from suspecting another Watergate or one of its many smaller-scale imitations, they expect the Churches also to put their cards openly on the table. Therefore by far the greater number of the many protests against the "Schillebeeckx case" (among others, the 60,000 who supported the national drive for signatures) called for a public and regulated procedure; they did so in the name of human rights and the credibility of the Gospel. But since this openness has not yet been achieved, we must at least make public such material as is actually available—material that is probably only the tip of a largely invisible iceberg.

This set of documents will also give some insight into the content and orientation of the objections raised by the central authorities and into their motives and arguments. The Roman documents are no longer the apodictic lists of "errors" which so many—and often no less prominent—predecessors of Schillebeeckx had to sign if they did not want to be excommunicated from the Church. In the "questionnaire" sent to Schillebeeckx arguments and reasons are given, and instead of assertions there are requests for clarification or explanation— even though at times the questions are obviously rhetorical. The third document, which is a reply to Schillebeeckx' answers, frequently resembles a regular scholarly discussion: the author, who is unnamed, often writes in the first person, cites fellow theologians in support of his argument, uses footnotes, and at times gives references to literature, such as one finds supplied, in reviews, for "the interested reader." Nonetheless it remains only too clear that in the final analysis the document is not a contribution to a discussion but a kind of set of demands.

The non-specialist reader will probably find the documents difficult going. The questions are put in the technical language of theology and, by and large, in the technical language of traditional Scholastic theology, which in our part of the world is hardly used anymore since the Council. Someone coming into contact with this language and type of argumentation for the first time will perhaps have difficulty in recognizing the Gospel—or the world of contemporary experience—in it. Especially since the days when, in the medieval universities, specialists had gained the upper hand, theology through the centuries had moved in the direction of an ever greater conceptual refinement. In the process there was an increasingly heavy emphasis on exact and abstract formulation. Only in recent decades have people come to realize almost everywhere—except, I am afraid, in Roman theology—that this emphasis on precision and clarity brings with it the serious danger of letting the real values of religious language slip through one's fingers. Religious language draws its power from extrapolated, metaphorical words and from symbols, for it realizes that in the final analysis the mystery cannot be comprehended or described directly. It is only to be seen "out of the corner of your eye" (Langdon Gilkey), and it slips out of the field of vision when you try to look straight at it. Religious experience cannot do without concepts and words, but the latter, it must always be realized, are essentially unsuited for authentic statements of faith: they are "analogical" and signify something only in virtue of their power to suggest images. It is therefore at least as important to gain a renewed awareness of this element of imagery in the objects of faith—for example, with the help of a related symbol—as it is to describe them in language that is as precise as possible (though even then always analogical). And in stating that, the historical component should be taken also into consideration. Even terms which at one time became official, such as, for example, the dogmatic statements of the first Christian centuries, fit into a pattern of language intelligible at the time but which in the course of the centuries (and in diverse cultures) has inevitably shifted and taken religious words along in the process.

In fact, in my opinion it is here—in the emphasis either on exact terminology or on images, i.e., either on the once fixed or on the historically changing element in the language of faith—that we have the real point of difference between traditional and modern theology and, therefore, between the Congregation for the Doctrine of the Faith and Schillebeeckx. This difference is the basis for the barrier to understanding of which I spoke earlier. Therefore even those who may find the questions of the Congregation to be "technical," abstract or cut off from the real world, and therefore unintelligible, nonetheless have grasped the real issue, which is one that in the final analysis concerns the entire ecclesial community.

In all this I have doubtless oversimplified the problem. After all, Schillebeeckx too uses language that is scholarly and therefore more remote language although his is derived more directly from the world of our present day experience. The characteristic difference between his technical language and that of the Congregation consists above all in the fact that by means of his technical language he is trying to "fill in" the symbols and once more make them intelligible and meaningful, instead of allowing them to go on being expressed in exact conceptual notions that are derived from a cultural pattern which is largely a thing of the past for us and that therefore has practically no meaning anymore. He wants to have us experience them "as new," and therefore he approaches them from unexpected angles—especially by an historical reconstruction of what their *original* fullness of meaning must have been. What was the overwhelming experience that led the friends of an executed, unorthodox rabbi to give him the weightiest names from their religious tradition: Messiah, Lord, Son of God? What was Jesus *himself* saying through the symbol "Father," so worn-out to us, when he used the word "Abba" with unparalleled intensity? In his pursuit of this purpose Schillebeeckx certainly does not underestimate the difficulty of remaining faithful, as a theologian, to the Church's tradition, which is our only access to the basic experience of the group around Jesus. Even though this tradition itself has also at times channeled the weighty symbols into technical, conceptual sentences and words which may make us forget that we are speaking of inconceivable mysteries, yet we cannot jump over this link to the past in our effort to plumb the original faith-experience of revelation. Schillebeeckx of his own accord asks for criticisms and—along with a great deal of approval—he has gotten them.[3] But he thought he could expect criticism that accepts his point of departure—which by and large is the point of departure for contemporary theology as a whole. The documents published here will show how far his expectation was fulfilled.

Finally, in addition to providing information on the secret procedure and a concrete introduction to the difference in point of departure between traditional ecclesiastical theology and a serious contemporary theology, the documents, especially Schillebeeckx' response, give a glimpse into the crucible of his publications. This is a welcome help to the understanding of his sometimes difficult line of argument. More than once we learn why he chose a certain interpretation or followed a certain expert. More importantly, he explains in a short compass not only how *Jesus: An Experiment in Christology* is constructed but also *why*. We read of what he was trying to achieve and how his method and purpose influenced the presentation of the content. In this choice, content and way of doing theology are essentially connected. This, once again, causes special difficulty for his Roman judges. His manner of proceeding is "unconventional," as he had already warned in his book. Various remarks of his censors show that this is in itself already a mark against him. At times paternally, at other times somewhat peevishly, they urge him to return to the familiar paths. At one point they even think they see him on the way back to the traditional terminology.

Only rarely have I read in a recent theological document so out-spoken a plea for the tried and true, the "old time religion" that at least disturbs no one. The Jesus of the Gospels—who more than any-one knew how to bring out the challenging and disconcerting, and thus Godward, power of traditional religious images—seems far away here. In the background an obvious basic conviction regarding his-torical development is at work, a conviction that is certainly not a dogma but is nonetheless posited without argument as a fixed point of reference, namely, that in the teaching of the Church, and especial-ly in official pronouncements, the content of the faith has found ex-pression once and for all in a specific terminology. In the course of the centuries the implications of this terminology have indeed been constantly explicitated and more accurately formulated, and that ter-minology does not need revision and renewal, even in the light of the authentic original Christian experience/revelation as contained in the New Testament. For in its content this experience/revelation now is, supposedly, identical with the teaching of the Church.

This basic conviction is to be seen as a variant of the much used model of continuous cultural progress (the prestige of this model, though, has dropped sharply in recent years). In fact it supposes, without any real justification being given, that the *theology* which is implied in the traditional statements of the Church is equally immu-table and inevitable. Apparently Roman theology is still unable to grasp the fact that language has meanwhile undergone a no less in-eluctable change, so that the old terms have fallen out of step with *us*, as it were, and need hermeneutical interpretation if they are to be un-derstood. As a result, the Congregation naively identifies its own the-ology with the teaching of faith, so that a real dialogue—in which *both* parties put their views up for discussion—is out of the question. With perfect logic, therefore, after the Declaration *Mysterium Ecclesiae* (which was written against him), Hans Küng was invited to a conver-sation in Rome, unless he *immediately* accepted the teaching contained in the document![4]

In any case, the old rule is apparently still in effect: a theologian may come out with something new only on condition that he can then show it is not new.[5]

It was principally for these three reasons that the board of edi-tors of *Tijdschrift voor Theologie* decided to publish the documents of the "Schillebeeckx case" in a Dutch translation, while also supplying the original French text in order to facilitate the most accurate judg-ment possible of a paradigmatic conflict between the teaching authority and theology in the Catholic Church. The publication is a logical consequence of our conviction—expressed as a reaction to the "Schillebeeckx case," among others, in the first issue of 1980—that theology also has a role as "disturber" of the ecclesial community; our concern for the authenticity and credibility of the faith imposes on us the task of propounding troublesome questions and critical answers. In a thematic issue to be published at the end of 1980 ("The Schillebeeckx Affair: Reflections and Reactions") we went more fully into the content of the documents and considered, among other things, their method and hermeneutic (T. J. van Bavel) and their image of the Church (B. Ad. Willems). A (religio-) psychological framework is also suggested within which the documents may be better understood (P. Vandermeersch, "Religion and the Need for Authority"), and there is a theological evaluation of a number of reactions to the "Schillebeeckx case." The accused author himself also took the opportunity to write an Afterword (E. Schillebeeckx).

In the present edition of the documents each is accompanied only by a few remarks intended to shed light on its context and significance. In the text itself obvious inaccuracies (in spelling or references) are corrected as a matter of course, unless the mistake is significant. Square brackets have been reserved for editorial remarks or for remarks introduced by the Roman censor into citations from Schillebeeckx' book.

In perusing these documents the reader must of course bear in mind that none of the authors—least of all the representatives of the Congregation!—were writing with an eye to publication. In addition, Schillebeeckx had to write his contribution in a foreign tongue, without the aid of a translator, as he himself notes. Thus even at the level of the language being used he was at a disadvantage, although the people in Rome thought they were making a concession by choosing French (the book *Jezus* has not been translated into French; in any case, the Dutch text was the basis for the discussion, a fact that at times seems to cause problems for the participants in the dialogue).

A notable difficulty in editing the translation of the documents seems to be that in a Christological context Schillebeeckx mostly uses not the strictly technical terms *godheid* (divinity) and *mensheid* (humanity, human nature), but *goddelijkheid* (divineness) and *menselijkheid* (humanness). Each of the latter two terms has a special nuance when used theologically: *goddelijkheid* seems to imply less than *godheid* (was this fact perhaps passed on to Rome by Dutch accusers?), while *menselijkheid* adds precisely a nuance of warmth and concreteness to the somewhat more formal term *mensheid*. Perhaps this last element is the reason why Schillebeeckx prefers *menselijkheid* (and, therefore, the parallel term, *goddelijkheid*). He has stated expressly that in using these terms he has no intention of detracting from the divine or human stature of Jesus.

Anyone who wants information on the course of events connected with the "investigation" may profitably turn to Peter Hebblethwaite's book, *The New Inquisition: The Case of Edward Schillebeeckx and Hans Küng* (New York, 1980), which also explains the procedure followed and conveys a good grasp of the themes under discussion and of their background. Of course, since Hebblethwaite did not have access to the official record published here, his reconstruction of the conversation in Rome is something of a tour de force. A special issue of *Archief van de kerken* 35 (1980), No. 14, July 9, 1980, 649–74 contains a number of noteworthy protests. Schillebeeckx' barely tolerated "advisor," B. van Iersel, provides a penetrating examination of the investigatory procedure and of the actual conversation in Rome.[6]

NOTES

1. Cf. B. van Iersel, "De onderzoeksprocedure van de congregatie voor de geloofsleer," *Tijdschrift voor Theologie* 20 (1980) 3–25, especially 6–10.

2. *Jesus: An Experiment in Christology,* tr. by H. Hoskins (New York, 1979), 575–82. See also, and especially, the studies collected in *The Understanding of Faith: Interpretation and Criticism,* tr. by N. D. Smith (New York, 1974), and the second volume of his "trilogy": *Christ: The Experience of Jesus as Lord,* tr. by John Bowden (New York, 1980), Part I of which deals with revelation and experience (27–79). Complements and nuances are given in *Interim Report on the Books Jesus and Christ,* tr. by J. Bowden (New York, 1981). These last two books were also brought into the "conversation" in Rome; cf. the Introduction to that document.

3. *Jesus,* 5. The book *Interim Report,* mentioned earlier, goes into a number of points in the criticisms that have been made; the reader will find there, among other things, many of the points raised in the documents published here, although in *Interim Report* they are treated in a much broader perspective.

4. The letter of the Congregation for the Doctrine of the Faith has been published (in English) by the United States Catholic Conference in *The Küng Dialogue: Facts and Documents* (Washington, D.C., 1980), 60–61.

5. In my book *A Survey of Catholic Theology, 1800–1970,* tr. by N. D. Smith (New York, 1970) I have gone into greater detail, especially regarding

the historical background of the tension between traditional neo-Scholastic theology and modern theology in the Catholic Church. But the years since have shown that the concluding section of that book, "Getting Used to the New Freedom," was much too optimistic. In my opinion, the basic substantive question has been very perceptively analyzed by Protestant theologian Langdon Gilkey in his *Catholicism against Modernity* (New York, 1975).

6. Originally in the article "De onderzoeksprocedure van de congregatie voor de geloofsleer," *Tijdschrift voor Theologie* 20 (1980) 3–25. Partial translations in German ("Wie fair was das Kolloquium mit Schillebeeckx?" *Orientierung* 44 /1980/ 42–45, and "Um den Rechtsschutz im römischen Lehrprüfungsverfahren," *ibid.* 52–56) and in French ("Le 'colloque Schillebeeckx' vu par un témoin," *Études*, 1980, 255–266).

CONGREGATION
OF FAITH
TO SCHILLEBEECKX

First Questions,
October 20, 1976

Introduction

The first document to reach Schillebeeckx via Cardinal Willebrands was signed by Cardinal Franjo Seper, Prefect of the Congregation for the Doctrine of the Faith. Like the subsequent documents, it carries the index number 46/66, from which Schillebeeckx infers that there has been a dossier on him since 1966 and that it still probably includes the material from the uncompleted "inquiry" of 1968. From the formal standpoint the document presented here is the result of the first twelve steps in the investigatory procedure: possible errors that have been found by experts and then acknowledged by Congregation and Pope are presented to the author in the form of "questions" for clarification (*Procedure*, art. 13). The document itself says that it is "normal" procedure to employ Cardinal Willebrands, Grand Chancellor of the University of Nijmegen, as intermediary. This statement is surely not beyond dispute; the general or regional superiors who serve as the "Ordinary" of the accused, or alternatively his own bishop, Msgr. Bluyssen, should have been informed.

As the document itself says in its Introduction, it is certainly not written in a spirit of ill will. It states that the Congregation really had to examine Schillebeeckx' work "as a result of the various reactions it has elicited," and the Congregation realizes that it has caused him pain (Conclusion). The style is at times paternalistic and shows a curial cumbersomeness ("How could the Congregation for the Doctrine of the Faith fail to be concerned?": II/C; "Why is it . . . that after the approval just indicated, a serious reservation must now be made?": III/B; the text is larded with "Reverend Father"). At other times, the document engages in subtle argumentation and indulges in the superior tone one finds in the traditional Scholastic book review ("One would need the eyes of a lynx to be able to ascertain that your book is proposing this defensible interpretation": II/A; note also the commentary inserted in brackets into passages cited from Schillebeeckx).

15

Traditional prejudices are displayed naively ("*Even* a great many Protestant exegetes recognize": II/D).

As far as content is concerned, the document is well organized: only after methodological questions have been raised does it turn to the historical and then the systematic theological content of Schillebeeckx' book. Its own position is clearly set forth (this is the strongest side of this kind of theology), with much of the explanation one remembers from good traditional manuals: on the concept of person, on person and nature in Christ, on the development of tradition and the meaning of the Church's pronouncements regarding the faith. At most one may ask whether no one in the Congregation realized that all this explanation is superfluous, and even somewhat insulting, for a theologian of Schillebeeckx' caliber (e.g., the explanation in II/A-5 that the humanity of Jesus suffers no *loss* by being actuated by a divine person instead of a human person—an age-old "solution" of an aporia by traditional Christology, but nonetheless an abstract postulate).

The drafters have a more difficult time of it when they have to define the role of historical research. Their point of departure is a very optimistic view of the continuous development of Christology in the New Testament and in later tradition, a development which they compare to a process of biological growth that guarantees homogeneity (I/A). By so proceeding, they intend to discredit, for example, Schillebeeckx' choice of "eschatological prophet" as the primordial interpretation of Jesus (II/B; cf. II/D, conclusion). Uninterpreted *theological* passages of the Bible, and even the words of consecration spoken in the liturgy, are used as an argument against an *historical* reconstruction (II/C, conclusion). Hermeneutics is taken to mean solely the "actualizing" of texts and therefore should come *after* exegesis. How uneasy the drafters are with the key concept of hermeneutics can be seen from the incidental phrase "in the normal sense of the term" (III/B; the passage has to do with the virginal conception of Jesus; the drafters do not understand how Schillebeeckx can doubt it "in a biological-material sense"—which is evidently considered to be the "normal" sense). The concern of the Congregation is clearly for "the objective value of language and of metaphysical concepts"; it finds distrust of these traits that are "rather widespread especially in contemporary Protestant [!] thought" (I/A-3).

In addition, some odd maneuvers occur in the argument. Several times an interview with Schillebeeckx (by J. Spitz, in *Kosmos & Oekumene* 8 [1974] no. 7) is used as a source, a practice at odds with art. 3 of the official regulations. Also used as though it were a piece of Schillebeeckx' own writing is his contribution to *Sept problèmes capitaux de l'Eglise* (Paris, 1969; English: Crucial Questions [New York, 1969]), although it is perfectly clear particularly in the French version (where the fact is noted as a running head on each page) that this too was a conversation ("*Entretien*").

It is also strange to see how, of all the texts that could have been used, the opening speech of John XXIII at Vatican II, in which the Pope surprised everyone with a call to "update" the Church's preaching, is chosen to back up the idea of the *im*mutability of doctrine, which, of course, the Pope did maintain as well. It is rather amusing, finally, to see a "sic" added twice to an expression of Schillebeeckx that the drafters regarded as strange ("*personnelle-humaine*"), which Schillebeeckx later points out was due to a mistaken translation on the part of the censor (III/A-1).

But the most striking thing of all is the identification, which is simply assumed, of the Congregation's own theological viewpoint with *the* ecclesial faith. Due to its principles, the Congregation cannot accept even the possibility of a genuinely different theology: the doctrine of faith *is identical with* the ecclesial pronouncements presently in use, these being understood in their "normal sense." This attitude—along with the official status of the Congregation—explains a number of characteristic utterances: Schillebeeckx is conceived as making a "concession" (II/E); he is urged *simply* to make his own once again the Christology "which *the Church* teaches its faithful" (II/A-5); the observation, which is not without a trace of smirking, that Schillebeeckx is really on the way back to the formulations of Chalcedon (III/A-1, after having first argued that Schillebeeckx' understanding of Christ's divinity must be either Monophysite or Nestorian!); and the appeal for an "unambiguously reassuring response" regarding the Church, for the sake of the "confused faithful" (III/C; cf. I/A-1).

What we are dealing with here, of course, are not simply questions asking for clarification; they contain at least an element of intimidation. Striking, on the other hand, is the assurance in the Conclusion that the Congregation too "is ready to change its interpretations and approaches as circumstances dictate." Is the reference to the understanding of Schillebeeckx' book or of the formulations of the faith? In any case, the hope is expressed that there may be a "greater or clearer unanimity."

The sequence of events will show whether or not this hope is realized.

THE QUESTIONNAIRE

Questions on the book
Jesus: An Experiment in Christology
addressed to the Reverend Edward Schillebeeckx, O.P.
by the Congregation for the Doctrine of the Faith

INTRODUCTION

Reverend Father, your book *Jesus: An Experiment in Christology* has now been added to a long series of works, a number of which have opened up very profitable paths for theological research. Your book is itself the product of considerable work carried on over many years, as is clear not only from its size but also from its detailed knowledge of contemporary studies on the problem of Jesus and from the uncommon power of synthesis that it shows.

Your purpose is to lead men and women of our day—even those who accept only such elements in the picture of Jesus as are supported by historical evidence—to the threshold of faith in "Jesus as that definitive saving reality which gives final point and purpose to [my] life" (30) or, in other words, to the threshold of faith in "salvation in Jesus coming from God" (557). You go still further and, at the end of your book, offer the outline of a Christology which, while taking into account the Christological creeds of the New Testament and of tradition, endeavors to accommodate itself to the intellectual horizon of contemporary man. Following this path, you come to recognize in God the Trinitarian fullness that is made up of the Father, the Son who appeared in Jesus, and the Spirit who animates the Church.

There is no doubt, Reverend Father, that you have produced this imposing work as a contribution to the expansion of Christ's reign.

18

For this reason the Congregation for the Doctrine of the Faith, which has found itself compelled to examine the book as a result of the various reactions it has elicited, has undertaken its task not only with care but with very sincere good will. Conscious as it is of acting as servant of the Vicar of Christ, how could the Congregation have had any other attitude toward a brother in the Church and in the priesthood? Its hope would certainly have been that it might be able to approve of the book without reservation.

Unfortunately, the Congregation has to say that it has found in your work many statements which cause it great bewilderment; some of these statements have to do with principles of methodology, others with the conclusions of exegetical study, others still with dogmatic theology. The questions involved are too serious for the Congregation to be able to evade its duty of telling you how it understands your thought and of asking you for clarifications. It is almost inevitable, after all, that despite diligent study, it has not always grasped all the nuances of your thinking; and even more serious misunderstandings are possible. It may be that the clarifications it asks of you will be able to clear up erroneous interpretations. It is obvious, of course, that your answers need not be limited to determinations regarding the meaning of your texts. As need dictates, they may further explain your thinking and add new points of view. They may also defend it against the objections raised to it.

This series of questions is being sent to you, Reverend Father, through His Eminence Cardinal Willebrands, Grand Chancellor of the University of Nijmegen. The Congregation for the Doctrine of the Faith is taking this course because it is the normal one. It is also glad to be able to take it because it is convinced that His Eminence, who is President of the Episcopal Conference of the Netherlands, will act as a peacemaker.

Section I.
Questions Regarding Methodology

A. Observations on the historical method used

1. *Preference given to particular currents in exegesis.*—In so vast an historical synthesis as is to be found in the second and third parts of your book, it is impossible that you should present the reader with a

personal study of every point in your inquiry. Rather, after a critical reading of the exegetes you are compelled to offer your own conclusions and, at least in a summary way, the reasons for the more important of these conclusions. By and large, this is what you have done. It is hard to deny, however, that you draw your inspiration (not always but clearly by preference) from the radical wing of Protestant scholarship. From the standpoint of a neutral observer, has not your failure to adopt views on which there is a broader consensus opened you to a greater risk of error? You are certainly not unaware that radical exegesis follows in large measure the methodological principle that preternatural interventions of God in the history of salvation are to be excluded. You are right, of course, not to be guided by an outdated exegesis and not to base your synthesis on views which are not sufficiently critical. But have you not gone to the opposite extreme and ended up with an overall vision of things that is likely to surprise a sizable number of able exegetes, Catholics especially but also Protestants, and almost all the exegetes of the Orthodox Churches—to say nothing of the general reader who, if he is a believer, will inevitably be confused?

2. *An excessive exegetical reduction?* Your exegetical synthesis often seems to be a reduction of texts to an undeniable kernel and a consequent elimination of even their substantive historical content as this has been generally maintained in Christianity.

A genetic reduction, which is concerned not to project more recent interpretation onto texts from the past, is undoubtedly legitimate and necessary. But if honesty requires that one not exaggerate the original historical datum, it also requires that one not excessively reduce it. Is it not prudent to think that there is a genuine continuity in the development of Christology in the New Testament Church which still had its eyes fixed on the person of its founder (this is a question which you yourself raise, 73–74)? Is it not reasonable to suppose that such a development is analogous to a biological process of growth (in which homogeneity persists amid progress) and does not consist of a series of heterogeneous additions or superpositions? Is it not better to respect the anticipated presence of the flower in the seed than so to reduce the latter that the flower becomes unintelligible? This general observation will have to be applied to particular cases (messianism, Son of Man, Servant of Yahweh, etc.) of which there will be question later on.

3. *A premature hermeneutic?* A hermeneutic, in the sense of an actualization of the Word in relation to contemporary spiritual and

philosophical currents, is legitimate; it is a "phase" of tradition. It must, however, follow upon exegesis and not be mingled with it. Are you certain that you have respected this principle in your discussion of the reign of God and the claims of Jesus? Judging from what you say (in this you resemble somewhat some Neo-Bultmannians), Jesus wanted to be a very abstract kind of functional figure, namely, the definitive messenger of God. But in the Judaism of the time eschatological expectations were generally focused on the figure of a King Messiah (sometimes on that of the Son of Man, that is, a transcendent Messiah); the idea of an eschatological prophet, who would not be this king or his forerunner or his associate, but to some extent a substitute for him, is hardly attested, and when it is, the attestation becomes the subject of debate. Is there not reason, then, to suspect that in this case the exegetes whom you follow have combined exegesis and hermeneutic?

There is all the more reason to be suspicious since the Jesus whom they discover fits in with certain characteristic traits that are rather widespread especially in contemporary Protestant thought: a tendency to distrust the objective value of language and of metaphysical concepts; a tendency to think of religious personages in functional terms that are stripped as far as possible of concrete details; a tendency to identify the cause of God with the cause of human beings. There is certainly no obligation to regard all these characteristics as permanent appropriations of philosophical thought.

(*Note.*—Important though these preliminary observations are, they admittedly do not directly touch the doctrines of faith. They will however be directly relevant in the exegetical matters to be considered further on. They are therefore not so much questions that already call for answers as they are considerations offered for reflection. But if you wish to give some response to them at this point, it will of course be welcome.)

B. Regarding Jesus of Nazareth as norm and criterion of all Christological interpretation (dogmatic methodology)

On a number of occasions, Reverend Father, you speak, on the one hand, of Jesus himself (or of "the offer" he made) and, on the other, of the acceptance of this "offer," an acceptance that is always an "interpretative response" and is found in Scripture, tradition, the teaching of the magisterium and the views of theologians. You even give the first section of your book a special title: "Jesus of Nazareth, Norm and Criterion of Any Interpretation of Jesus" (43).

This is how you explain this title: "The starting-point for any Christology or Christian interpretation of Jesus is not simply Jesus of Nazareth [since—is not this what you mean?—he cannot be reached in an immediate way], still less the Church's *kerygma* or creed [since—once again, is this not your meaning?—these are already "interpretative responses"]. Rather it is the movement which Jesus himself started in the first century of our era; more particularly because this Jesus is known to us, historically speaking, only via that movement. . . . In other words, the starting-point is the first Christian community—but as a reflection of what Jesus himself was, said and did" (44).

If this is the case, it seems that we are to find the norm and criterion of all interpretations of Jesus in the New Testament writings (especially the Gospels). These documents are approached, however, not precisely in terms of what they intend to teach, but as means of getting back—as far as this is possible by historical study—to Jesus of Nazareth himself or to his "offer"; thus you write: "What that offer [of salvation] was we can infer only indirectly from the reactions and other evidences recorded in the New Testament" (44). In the final analysis, then, the norm and criterion of any interpretation of Jesus is the Jesus of whom we have historical knowledge.

Does not such an approach give rise to the following objection? The approach is valid in the demonstrations proper to fundamental theology (insofar as this deals with the origins of Christianity); in the realm of faith and dogmatic theology, on the other hand, the absolute norm of our assents and reflections is Scripture, tradition, and what are called the "definitive" judgments of the Church's magisterium. This norm will certainly never contradict the sure findings of history, but it may and in fact does go beyond these. Yet it seems, Reverend Father, that for you the norm and criterion of all interpretations of Jesus is in every area (even the realm of the creeds and dogmatic theology) the Jesus knowable by historical means. This interpretation of your thought seems valid not only because you nowhere suggest the distinction that has been made here, but also and above all because of what will be set forth in the next section (C).

(*Note.*—You do, of course, think that account should be taken of the teaching of Scripture and the Church when the effort is being made to offer new Christological interpretations; but you do not seem to regard this teaching as providing norms which determine once and for all the meaning of the objects of faith.)

C. Regarding the "offer" of Jesus and the "interpretative responses" to it (dogmatic methodology)

What was the "offer" of Jesus? He proclaimed the reign of God, and "in its fullness ... Jesus' message of God's lordship and his kingdom is: God's universal love for men as disclosed in and through his [Jesus'] actual mode of conduct, consistent with and consequent upon it, and thus as an appeal to us to believe in it and hope for this coming salvation and kingdom of peace, 'imported by God' [with a perspective opening to what lies beyond our present life], and likewise faithfully to manifest its coming in a consistent way of living: the praxis of the reign of God" (154).

In order to get this same point across, you had originally planned, as you tell your readers, to give your book the title: "Salvation in Jesus Coming from God" (557), and you use still other formulations to convey the same meaning, for example: "Jesus acts ... as the eschatological [that is, supreme and definitive] prophet from God" (245).

Faith is the response to this "offer" of Jesus. The initial "response" of faith is already, it seems, an interpretation of the life of Jesus (including the paschal events). But this response is so close to the "offer" itself that you designate it "the given factor" (665) and you use the same expressions for it as for the "offer" itself. You say, in fact: "I believe [this confession is, at least approximately, the first response of faith] in Jesus as that definitive saving reality which gives final point and purpose to my life" (30). Other responses followed upon the first, both in the New Testament and throughout the history of the Church (especially in the great Christological councils); these developed in new ways the interpretative dimension of the faith.

In accordance with "contemporary history of culture," you distinguish, Reverend Father, between "first-order assertions," which are fundamental and "almost immutable," and "second-order assertions," which perceptibly change because they are dependent on the horizons of understanding found in various cultures. You add that these "second-order assertions" are either "conjunctural" and change only slowly, or "ephemeral" and liable to change easily and quickly (576–78).

This is meant as clarification of your statement that "the first response of faith," which acknowledges Jesus "as definitive salvation given to human beings," is a "first-order assertion" (549), whereas subsequent responses and the understanding of Jesus himself in whom the definitive saving action of God is accomplished belong to the class of "second-order assertions" (*ibid.*).

This implies that you seem to regard every Christology which is not purely functional and which does not consider Jesus solely in his function as supreme and definitive messenger of God, as liable to change in greater or lesser degree and as possessing only a more or less relative value. Is not this the reason why you say that if one holds "that in Jesus God saves men" one maintains "a primary and fundamental Christian orthodoxy" (*ibid.*)? And are you not making the same point when you say: "As a believer, one is bound by whatever Jesus entails, not directly by those articulating concepts" (318)? In an interview published some years back (in: Y. Congar, J. Daniélou, *et. al.*, *The Crucial Questions on Problems Facing the Church Today* [New York: Paulist, 1969], 64) you had already stated: "The dynamic of faith's understanding is essentially both 'demythologizing' (dissolving the previous formulations of faith) and 'remythologizing' (constructing ever new formulations of faith)." This statement gives the impression that the mutability of "interpretative responses" is extensive indeed and can never cease. And in fact in your book on Jesus you come out in favor of doctrinal changes the importance of which may not be minimized and which in their turn are essentially provisional: "Christology and Trinity, redemption, grace and original sin, Church and sacraments, prayer and 'the last things' (eschatology): it all seems no longer what we all used to take for granted. . . . I do not begrudge any believer the right to describe and live out his belief in accordance with old models of experience, culture and ideas. But this attitude isolates the Church's faith from any future and divests it of any real missionary power to carry conviction with contemporaries for whom the Gospel is—here and now—intended. Obviously, the new models will in turn be replaced by others" (581–82).

(*Note.*—It is a fact that various of the points you mention here—original sin, for example—pose difficult problems today. But these must be resolved without abandoning the meaning which the teachings of Scripture and the Church have consciously proposed for our belief.)

The Congregation for the Doctrine of the Faith maintains that the carefully circumscribed meaning which Scripture or the "definitive" declarations of the Church have intended to impose on faith is capable (in principle) of being discerned. The Congregation also maintains that this meaning, while it does not exhaust the truth of the mysteries and is grasped in a manner that is subjectively very imperfect—by way of negation and excellence, as the Scholastics put it—is nonetheless unqualifiedly true and therefore remains unchangeable. This view of the matter has been authoritatively set forth by Vatican Council I (*AAS* [1962], 972 [sic: ed.]), by Pope John XXIII (*AAS* 54 [1972 (sic: 1962, ed.)] 792), and in the Declaration *Mysterium Ecclesiae* of the Congregation for the Doctrine of the Faith (*AAS* 65 [1973] 401–04). Is it possible, Reverend Father, to reconcile your ideas on "second-order assertions" and their mutability with this view of the matter?

SECTION II.
QUESTIONS REGARDING THE QUEST OF THE HISTORICAL JESUS

A. A starting-point: Jesus as a human person

At the beginning of your book, Reverend Father, you say that for you the "starting-point" of all your thinking is "the man Jesus, in the sense of 'a human person' " (33); and you later speak on various occasions of this human person, Jesus (e.g., 655–56, 667–68). (*Note.*—This "starting-point," which is made explicit in your introduction, seems to inspire both your exegesis and your systematic theology. This is why it is being considered here, although in an effort to understand it we have been compelled to have recourse not only to your glossary [745–46] but also to passages in your systematic essay [667–68].)

When you refer to this "starting-point," is your intention to say simply that Jesus possesses a genuine, intelligent and free human subjectivity, while not denying that this subjectivity, far from having the final say, is in continuity with an ultimate subjectivity, that of the eternal Word? It would be possible to interpret in this manner the expression "a humanly conscious center of action and human ... freedom" (667) which you apply to Jesus of Nazareth. There would then be question not of an ultimate "center," an ultimate, closed subjectivity, but of a subjectivity that is perhaps simply proximate and that opens upon an ultimate subjectivity, which is the transcendent "I" of the divine Word. If this be the meaning, then your statement is defensible, despite its form which is confusing as compared with that of the corresponding statement in the teaching of the Church. The latter takes "person" as ultimate subject and therefore speaks, in the case of Christ, of a divine person who has assumed not a human person but a concrete humanity, the human nature of Jesus.

Unfortunately, one would need the eyes of a lynx to be able to say that your book is proposing this defensible interpretation. On the other hand, when you set yourself to give a formal definition of person, you say only that it is a "complete (*afgerond*), independent (*zelfstandig*), self-subsistent (*op zich staande*) existence" (745). In this passage you speak of the person as the Church does in its Christological teaching: A person is an ultimate intellectual subject.

(*Note.*—In your definition you are certainly speaking of a being endowed with intelligence and freedom. This you presuppose, or perhaps you actually express it (in accordance with a terminology often used nowadays), when you use the word "existence."—When you come to speak of the Blessed Trinity, you also emphasize the intersubjective relations implied by the idea of person. This causes little difficulty, but it is of secondary importance in connection with the present issue.)

Person as you define it can be considered in two ways. *First*, from the standpoint of its *constitutive elements* (those that define it). When thus considered, the person, in us (but not in Christ), is identical with our human substance, our individual, self-enclosed human nature. *Second*, the person, because it is a subject, can be considered from the standpoint of *what it possesses*, whether it is inherent, by assumption or even by external acquisition. In this way our person can be called healthy or sick, rich or poor.

According to the Council of Chalcedon (*DS* 301f.), Christ, the Son of God, is a single person who is consubstantial with the Father according to his divinity. For this reason we say that from the standpoint of the constitutive elements of the person he is a divine person. But according to that same Council, he was born within time according to his human nature. For this reason, even though he is not a human person as far as the constitutive elements of person are concerned, we may say, speaking absolutely, that he is a human person from the standpoint of what he possesses through the assumption of his humanity. (The expression "human person" is nonetheless usually avoided, because it easily suggests an erroneous view of Christ.) The Fourth Lateran Council, speaking of the person from the standpoint of its constitutive elements, says: "[The Son of God, Jesus Christ, is] one person in two natures" (*DS* 800).

Given your definition of a person, in what sense, Reverend Father, do you call Christ a human person? Unfortunately, a number of your Christological statements must, it seems, be understood as meaning that Jesus is a human person because his humanity contains within it all the elements constitutive of a person. If this be the case, then

Christ is not a divine person in two natures (*DS* 800). The Christology professed for centuries in the Church has been abandoned.

Here are some examples of the statements in question:

1. In your Christology you defend the idea of a certain "identity" [in Jesus] between "a finite personal-human mode of being" and "a divine, infinite (and thus analogous) mode of 'being person' " (667). This seems to mean that the humanity of Jesus as a person and the Word of God as a person (in an analogous sense) form a unity—of which there will be question further on.

2. You also explain that in Christ there is "a deepening, mutual *enhypostasis* [in the sense of a reception, an inclusion, in a person], with the resurrection as its climactic point" (667). But if we are to be able to think of such a "deepening, mutual *enhypostasis*" must we not admit that in him there are two persons united, the person of the Word and the person of the humanity of Jesus?

3. You explain the term "*an*hypostasis" as follows: "An-hypostasis (*an* = 'non-,' or 'not') indicates a condition from which 'being-a-human-person' is absent; it is implied [this is the traditional teaching of the Church] that Jesus does indeed have a human nature and (in that sense) is a human being, but that his being-*qua*-person is constituted by the divine person [of the Word]" (746). This is accurate, but you add, by way of criticism: "[If the person of Christ is so understood, it follows] that Christ is not a human person." *Remark:* This consequence (which offends you), namely, that "Christ is not a human person," may mean simply that in his humanity he does not have all the constitutive elements of a person, where "person" means ultimate subject. This consequence, which is fully in accord with the formula of the Fourth Lateran Council: "One [divine] person in two natures" (*DS* 800), does not satisfy you.

4. Therefore you go on to say: "This at any rate suggests that Christ is not a human being 'complete and unabridged' " (746). *Remark:* Traditional teaching, on the contrary, says that Jesus is fully a man, that is, an ultimate subject who possesses humanity. This ultimate subject is the Word of God, who possesses a humanity (a human nature) in the full sense.

5. Finally, you say that in "current Christology" attempts are made (in various ways, to be sure) to explain "the en-hypostasis without an-hypostasis: that is, Jesus suffers no deprivation of human personal being and yet is one with the Son of God" (*ibid.*). *Remark:* We perceive from this passage that this is in fact the project of a host of

contemporary theologians and that you are in favor of this project. But the humanity of Jesus, united to the person of the Word of God, suffers no *loss* from being actuated by a divine person instead of simply being a human person.

Can one fail to see, Reverend Father, that your statements about Jesus as a human person depart from the Christological tradition of the Church? Do you think that a new horizon of understanding requires this departure—one that is admittedly concerned with subtleties but that is also pregnant with consequences?

A final remark.—It has not escaped the notice of the Congregation for the Doctrine of the Faith that at least on one occasion you mute your assertion of a human person in Christ. You say that we must not "without all sorts of qualifications" or "simply and solely" assert that Jesus is a human person, for while he stands "over against (*tegenover*)" the Father [and the Spirit, ed.] he does not stand "over against" the Son (667). We may interpret: He can address the Father, but not the Son, as a "Thou." In this passage you have put your finger on a real and important difference. If you were to spell out the "all sorts of qualifications" to be made in speaking of Jesus as a human person, would you not perhaps be led simply to make your own once again the Christology which the Church teaches its faithful? At present, however—unless we misunderstand you—there are too many statements pointing in the opposite direction to permit the judgment that you have reached this goal. In any case, we are happy to find in your pages an admission which may be promising.

B. Jesus (it is said) presented himself not as Messiah but as eschatological prophet

In agreement with Wrede, whose thesis was taken over by Bultmann and after him by exegetes who while separating themselves from him have remained under the influence of his radical criticism, you think, Reverend Father, that Jesus did not wish to play the part of the Messiah King whom the prophets had foretold (245). We have no trouble in granting that he did not wish to be a king in the political sense of the term. From this it does not follow, however, that he did not intend to bring to fulfillment a messianic synthesis in which a number of Old Testament eschatological figures—including the central one, the figure of the Messiah King—would have their place: The Messiah would reign but in a manner that is religious and full of mystery. You do not accept that Jesus conceived the synthesis which the early Church attributed to him and which, while supposing him to have possessed a profound originality (is it, however, more understandable to assign such originality to his disciples?), locates him nonetheless within the horizon of understanding proper to his time. You prefer to attribute to Jesus himself only the project—which had very little historical flesh to it—of being "the eschatological prophet from God" (245). People at that time admittedly did expect eschatological prophets who would be forerunners or assistants of the Messiah, and even an eschatological prophet who would also be the Messiah King (Jn 6:14f). But in the literature of the time the idea of a final prophet who would not be a king but would instead be a substitute as it were for the Messiah King appears only vaguely or as a very secondary notion (J. Coppens, *Le messianisme royal* [Paris, 1974]; *idem*, *Le messianisme et sa relève prophétique* [Gembloux, 1974]; S. van der Woude and M. de Jonge, "chrio," *TDNT* 9:509–20; cf. Jn 1:20f; 7:40f, 52).

However much we may be tempted, there can be no question here of entering into a historical discussion of your position; that kind of discussion would have to be quite extensive. But if we take as our standpoint the teaching of the faith, the disturbing conclusion from your thesis of the absence of any messianic project on the part of Jesus is that there is no real continuity in the history of salvation. We are justified in judging rather that the messianic expectation of the Old Testament has been frustrated: Jesus is no longer the "Amen" (Rev 3:14; cf. 2 Cor 1:10) who fulfills all the prophetic promises but at a higher level. Is this not a serious matter? And is it any less serious a matter to claim that Jesus himself awaited the messianic figure of the Son of Man, with whom he did not identify himself (148, 472), whereas the early Church and the Church of later centuries as well have believed in Jesus as Messiah and Son of Man?

C. *Regarding Jesus as Servant of Yahweh, handed over for our sins*

It is your view, Reverend Father, that in none of the predictions of his passion did Jesus refer to his death as sacrificial and propitiatory (311). In order to be able to maintain this position, you must refuse to attribute to Jesus certain *logia* which enjoy a better fate in the hands of many exegetes. More serious still, you are led to deny even that the words of eucharistic institution, as far as those elements in them are concerned which are common to Paul and the Synoptics, can be regarded as historical (308).

Nonetheless the substantial historicity of these words is certified by solid arguments, especially the one provided by Paul's words: "I received as coming from the Lord [this would be the normal translation of *apo tou kyriou*] what I in turn passed on to you" (1 Cor 11:25). Many of the best contemporary exegetes emphasize the significance of these words. You, on the other hand, take no account of this argument or of many others put forward by truly critical scholars; instead you rally to the opinion of W. Marxsen, who may be counted among the most radical of the Protestant exegetes. As you see it, there is nothing historical in the New Testament accounts of the Last Supper, except the fact of the supper itself with its last sharing of a cup as a sign of union in the Kingdom despite the imminent death of the Master, and except for the *logion* of Jesus about not drinking the fruit of the vine again, save (but in this qualification you see a borrowing from another saying of the Lord) in the Kingdom of God. How could the Congregation for the Doctrine of the Faith fail to be concerned that your exegesis seems to remove the historical foundation from essential Christian convictions about the Eucharist?

But the issue transcends the mystery of the Eucharist. If Jesus as known by history is the norm and criterion of any Christology (cf. above, Section I B) and if he manifested no intention of offering his life as a propitiatory sacrifice, does it not follow that we are not bound by the sacrificial soteriology of the New Testament and Christian tradition? Should we be surprised, then, that in the fourth part of your book, in which you present your outline of a Christology, you say nothing to suggest a sacrificial soteriology, and this despite your central idea of "salvation in Jesus coming from God" (557)? In a conversation concerning your book on Jesus (published in a recent little book which was edited by you and H. M. Kuitert: *Jezus van Nazareth en het heil van de wereld* [Baarn, 1975]), you summed up your thinking on the death of Jesus. This summary neatly pulls together what you say in scattered passages of your book. Here is the content of your thinking: "First, I would dare to say that we are saved *despite* the death of Jesus, in spite of it! I would add only that such language is in the final analysis somewhat inadequate. For God is not checkmated by what men—not God himself—did to Jesus, namely, put him to death. God is greater and more powerful than the powerlessness of this death. Moreover, Jesus gave a *positive content* to the negativity of his death by his love for his Father and for human beings. This is why God sustains him even through the negativity of death. Thus we are really brought to salvation in the love of Jesus and through this love-unto-death. In the resurrection, the negativity present in this death is overcome by the saving power of God" (39).

But Scripture and tradition contain an essential teaching of which this passage says nothing. According to Scripture and tradition God willed the obedience of Jesus unto death as a sacrifice by which he might make reparation for our rebelliousness. St. John, for example, writes: "In this is love, not that we loved God but that he loved us and sent his Son to be the expiation for our sins" (1 Jn 4:10); and St. Paul: "[God] did not spare his own Son but gave him up for us all" (Rom 8:32). How is your statement that God did not hand Jesus over to death to be harmonized with this assertion of the Apostle, which belongs to the core of the mystery? And what are we to think of this view which you propose in your book, "that—not comprehending it, perhaps, but as a heartfelt conviction—he [Jesus] integrated this death into his proffer of salvation, the point and purpose of his whole life" (542)? "Not comprehending it, perhaps": How is this compatible with the words which for almost twenty centuries priests have spoken in the eucharistic anamnesis, putting them on the lips of Jesus?

The sacrificial and propitiatory offering of Christ is indeed a mystery that bedazzles the mind. But when prudently understood and accepted in faith, it is the privileged locus at which today as in the past the unfathomable depths of God's love are revealed. No one will eliminate it from the Church's creed (cf. *DS* 1751, 1753; Vatican Council II, Constitution *Sacrosanctum Concilium*, no. 47).

D. *Concerning Jesus and God his Father*

Even a great many Protestant exegetes recognize that Jesus departed from the Jewish usage of his day and distinguished himself from his examiners by speaking, with regard to himself, of "my Father," and, with regard to them, of "your [sing., pl.] Father." (Only in the *Pater* [Matthew's version], a prayer which Jesus was teaching his disciples to say, does the expression "our Father" occur.)

Recent studies, especially those of Professor J. Jeremias, have reached the following conclusions: at least on several occasions Jesus addressed God as *Abba*. In everyday speech, this mode of address was used, with few exceptions, only by children—young or grown-up—in speaking to their own father. Finally, as far as prayer is concerned, Jewish texts from the time of Jesus Christ provide no example of an Israelite addressing God as *Abba*. (The few texts from Hellenistic Judaism in which God is invoked as Father do not lessen the significance of this fact.) For your part, Reverend Father, you believe that in "a few cases (which point of course to a new tendency)" (260) *Abba* was in fact used as a religious *invocation*. But you give no references for this statement and, if we are to judge by the very careful studies made of the point, it would probably be difficult for you to provide any. In any case, the practice of Jesus was singularly unusual and, if the Master led his disciples to adopt it in their turn, even in the Hellenistic communities (Gal 4:4–6; Rom 8:15), they must have been conscious of acting with a holy daring which only their union with Christ could justify (cf. the passages just cited).

All things considered, the way in which Jesus speaks of his Father and to his Father manifests an awareness of a filial union with God which is at once unparalleled and yet can in some measure be shared.

Are you not worried, Reverend Father, at having decidedly minimized the real situation when you write: "Thus that Jesus should say *Abba* to God—apart from the great solemnity, holding God at a distance from men, with which people in Jesus' time used to pray to him [would this have been true of the recitation of the psalms?]—makes no essential difference" (259)? You do, however, say that the experience which Jesus had of God as *Abba* was "the soul, source and ground of Jesus' message, praxis and ministry as a whole" (266); that it therefore "evidently goes deeper than the purely prophetic consciousness" (*ibid.*); and that it begins "to prompt *theological* questions" (*ibid.*).

But if by his attitude to his *Abba* Jesus pointed, indirectly as it were, to a sonship that was peculiarly his own, did he not manifest and further specify this in other ways as well? Yes, he manifested it by attributing to himself prerogatives of a divine kind which did not however prevent his giving himself completely to his heavenly Father and to his brothers and sisters. He also manifested it, according to many texts of the Synoptics (texts which are debated but which for various reasons deserve to be taken into consideration), by indicating that he was the Son of the Father (for example, in the text appropriately called a "hymn of jubilation," in the parable of the murderous vineyard workers, and in a verse of the eschatological discourse in Mark and Matthew).

In regard to these texts (their historical value and their meaning) you adopt positions more negative than those of various renowned exegetes, not only Catholic but also Protestant. How is it that while granting that Jesus manifested through his actions the consciousness he had of himself, you can say that he "never posited himself (beside the Kingdom of God) as the second object of his preaching" (258)? This is, of course, a kind of dogma for a certain type of criticism. But should you subscribe to it?

When all is said and done—and this is the point that matters in the eyes of the Congregation for the Doctrine of the Faith—the Jesus of history, as you conceive him, seems to provide but a weak basis for the Christology developed in the New Testament and later in the tradition of the Church. The Constitution *Dei Verbum* (no. 19) of the Second Vatican Council looks for more solid results from a sound historical study of the Gospels. This is a point that should set us thinking.

E. Regarding Easter as a turning point

You affirm, Reverend Father, the "personal and bodily resurrection" of Jesus (645); this acceptance can only be a cause for rejoicing. But what you say about the signs of this resurrection, especially the empty tomb and the appearances, is upsetting. You do not go so far as to deny the discovery of the empty tomb, but you avoid asserting it. And the least that can be said is that you have not tried to assay the historical arguments which even in the eyes of many critics still retain their value.

As regards the appearances, which you challenge as psychological (and in this sense historical) realities, do you not treat too lightly many explicit texts among which 1 Corinthians 15:3–8 is especially important because it is so early? Moreover, in (more or less) reducing the apparition narratives to conversion experiences do you not unduly lump together two kinds of experience which are in fact very different? According to the New Testament, conversion (the vocabulary of which, in any case, is pretty much absent from the appearance stories) is required of *every* believer; it is not especially characteristic of the apostles and the first disciples. The appearance narratives, on the contrary, give expression in their own way to *a specific, "foundational" testimony* which only the disciples of the first hour rendered. The series of Easter appearances therefore *ended* rather soon both by right and in fact, whereas conversion is a "permanent" requirement in the Church. Your statement that the words of Jesus in the Gospel of Matthew: "Where two or three are gathered in my name, there am I in the midst of them" (18:20) are "perhaps the purest, most adequate reflection of the Easter experience" (646) has probably no chance of being accepted save by a very small number of exegetes.

It is true that in a recent colloquium (H. M. Kuitert and E. Schillebeeckx, *op. cit.*, 51f) you soften somewhat the bluntness of your position. You allow that the grace of conversion (a grace of which the disciples, you had already said, were beneficiaries) may have stimulated, by way of consequence, "some visual element," but you attach no importance to such "concomitant phenomena." The concession made is minimal.

Given your conception of the matter, how can you explain the fact that the disciples were convinced not only that their Master lived on somehow in glory but specifically that he had experienced a resurrection in the course of history, although it took him into the next world? The Jews did not attribute such a resurrection to any of the patriarchs, to any of the ancient prophets or to any king; they did not think of attributing it even to the Messiah. Resurrection into the world beyond was rather generally accepted under the influence of the Pharisees, but only as part of the events that would bring the present course of the world to an end.

SECTION III.
QUESTIONS REGARDING THE SYSTEMATIC THEOLOGY OF THE BOOK

A. Regarding the mysteries of the Incarnation and the Trinity

1. *The Incarnation.*—As was said earlier (Section II A), the Incarnation is the mystery of "one person [the Son of God] in two natures [divinity and humanity]" (*DS* 800): The eternal Son of God, assuming a human nature, is born of the Virgin Mary. Classical theology gives the name "hypostatic union" to this union of the human nature of Jesus with his divine person.

In connection with your idea of Jesus as a human person (cf. above, Section II A), you prefer to speak, Reverend Father, of a " 'hypostatic identification' without *anhypostasis*" (667), that is, an identification of the human person of Jesus and his divine person. "This man, Jesus," you explain, "within the human confines of a (psychologically and ontologically) personal-human [French: "personnelle-humaine (sic)"] mode of being, is identically the Son, that is, the 'Second Person' of the Trinitarian plenitude" (*ibid.*).

This conception of things raises two serious questions. *First*, do you not alter the specific meaning of the dogma itself when you thus replace the idea of *one* person in two natures with the idea of an identification of *two* persons? Such an alteration cannot be accepted by the Church (cf. above, Section I C).

Second: In your opinion there is either (this is a *first hypothesis*) an identity in the strict sense (excluding all real distinction) between the person of the Word and the human person (as you call it) of Jesus. If this first hypothesis is accepted, it seems impossible to avoid monophysism, inasmuch as the nature (the *physis*) is included as a constituent of the person. Or else (and this is a *second hypothesis*) what is meant is not an identity in the strict sense but only an ineffable union of two persons. In this case, a kind of Nestorianism would be unavoidable: two persons really distinct but forming a supreme union. It would then be possible to say that "Jesus, within the confines of a . . . personal-human mode of being, is identically the Son, the 'Second Person' of the Trinitarian plenitude" (cf. the text cited just above). But the adverb "identically" would then be used loosely because of the loose identity which it expresses. (*Note.*—In dealing with this question you seem to use now "identification," now "identity," without distinction.)

Which of these two hypotheses reflects your thinking? At times you seem to speak of an identity in the strict sense; but passages bearing the contrary meaning seem to be in the majority.

We may cite first a passage which seems to envisage a strict identity: "An identity of a finite personal-human [French: "personnelle-humaine (sic)"] mode of being and a divine, infinite (and thus *analogous*) mode of 'being person' is no contradiction, since the ground of the distinction between the creature and God lies not in the perfection of the creature but in its finitude, while all that is positive in it is yet totally 'derived' [?] from God" (667). (*Note.*—This argument is by no means secure against attack. For, in the essence of creatures or in the constitution of created persons, there is no real distinction between a perfection that would be derived from God and a finitude. There are only *degrees of participation* which are entirely, and with complete necessity, really distinct from unparticipated Being. But we may leave this point aside.)

We may cite now two passages which seem to require a close union rather than a strict identity. *First passage:* You speak of an "*en*hypostasis" (a certain inclusion in a person) which was "deepening" and "mutual" during the life of Jesus prior to the paschal mystery, and reached its "climactic point" in the resurrection (667). Does not the idea of a *mutual* and *increasing en*hypostasis between two terms exclude a strict identity between them? *Second passage:* In a colloquium on the subject of your book (published by J. Spitz in *Kosmos & Oekumene* 8 [1974], 185), you express yourself as follows: "The Christology of about a decade ago, which is still set forth in preaching, is no longer persuasive. People now resist the Christ of worship whom the Churches present to them in such an exaggeratedly divinized form. I too am puzzled by this approach. It is not that I deny the divinity of Jesus, but I too find great difficulty with *this harsh and ruthless identification: Jesus = God.*"—But is it possible to conceive a more unqualified identification of Jesus with God than that which denies any real distinction between the person of the Word and the (so-called) human person of Christ?

We shall give up trying to choose between the two hypotheses. Perhaps your thinking wavers between them, as between Scylla and Charybdis. And—who knows?—perhaps this wavering is preparing the way for a rediscovery of Chalcedon?

2. *The Most Blessed Trinity.*—From the experience which Jesus had of God as *Abba* and from this experience considered as being concretely the core of his life and message, you conclude, Reverend Father, that the human reality of Christ was in its very constitution a relation to God as Father. You go on to explain this relation as resulting from "the unique turning of the Father himself to Jesus" (658). You say something of the same kind when you speak of the Spirit who lives in the Church (660). In these divine "turnings" to the human reality of Jesus and to the Church you thus see the persons of the Son and the Spirit. You think that these persons are eternal and not contingent, although the terms of their activity are intrinsically contingent and temporal: "God," you say, "would be no God without creatures and Jesus of Nazareth" (668).

You certainly cannot fail to see, Reverend Father, that the passage from Jesus of Nazareth to the mystery of the Trinity, when made as you make it, raises a series of problems, some of which have received the attention of the magisterium: source of the distinction between the divine persons, cf., e.g., *DS* 1330; God and creation, cf., e.g., *DS* 3035. But let us not dwell on these points. The important thing here—now that in recent years some Catholic theologians have doubted or even denied the eternal existence of the Trinity in God—

the really important thing is that you accept this existence without equivocation.

B. *Regarding the virginal conception of Jesus*

Why is it, Reverend Father, that after the approval just indicated, a serious reservation must now be made? The question now is of a truth of our religion which may be called peripheral but which the Church has never ceased to teach to believers and which helps reveal the heart of God to us.

Despite the place of honor which the Gospels of Luke and Matthew give to the virginal conception of Jesus in their infancy narratives, you cast doubt on it—at least, to use your own words, if the virginal conception is taken in "a biological-material sense" (554). But the virginal conception of Jesus, which reaches beyond the realm of the biological by reason of its religious and Christological dimension, does nonetheless have a biological aspect, which is described in the Constitution *Lumen gentium:* "She [Mary] gave birth on earth to the very Son of the Father, not through the knowledge of man (*et quidem viri nescia*)" (no. 62 [63, ed.]). Must you not acknowledge that language is being abused when someone would have it thought that the virginal conception of Jesus could be understood in a non-biological sense, that is, *cum concursu viri* [with the cooperation of a male]?

In any case, the tradition of the Church has sanctioned the scriptural data as referring to the virginal conception of Jesus in the normal sense of the term. The Lateran Council that was celebrated in 649 under the leadership of Pope Martin I teaches this in an especially authoritative manner (*DS* 503). The virginal conception is also taught in the Constantinopolitan Creed which the Church unceasingly professes: "He was conceived of the Holy Spirit; he was born of the Virgin Mary."

You take up this question chiefly in terms of objections. Have you not approached it in a quite one-sided manner, and have you said what ought to be said?

C. *Regarding the Church*

In your book, Reverend Father, you say hardly anything about the Church, and the subject with which you are dealing only partially justifies this reticence. At most you discuss the calling of the disciples closest to Jesus (218–29) and, not without reservation, the calling of the Twelve (389, 421). But in a recent interview on the subject of your book, you said: "I retain a sense of solidarity with the Church. What I have utterly lost, however, is any sense of union (*verbondenheid*) with the Vatican. This Vatican, with its Congregations which are like so many extensions of the Pope—this used to mean something to me at one time, but not anymore. If only the Vatican were restructured, with the Pope and some associates acting as a kind of final court of appeal in the Church, while authority was invested directly in the episcopal conferences. . . . There should be a final authority to which appeal may be made, but nothing more than that. [An authority] which, for the sake of Christian and Catholic world opinion, would be able to issue a reprimand: What you are doing is no longer Christian. . . . I would insist on a place for the Pope, but in that form. Even from the ecumenical point of view this is important" (J. Spitz, ed., in *Kosmos & Oekumene* 8 [1974], 190).

In the same interview you say that your book is an attempt to express the heart of the Christian message and that this leads to "a certain relativization of the ecclesiastical institution" (*ibid.*). We certainly must not take too seriously what is said in the free and sometimes exaggerated language of an interview. But neither can we simply pass it over in silence. Such statements (which have been published) confuse the faithful and manifest to some degree a way of thinking. Can you provide an unambiguously reassuring response with regard to the hierarchical constitution of the Church?

A Few Words in Conclusion

The preceding pages have been many. This is due in part to the many requests for clarification that are made, but it is due above all to the explanations which accompany the questions. It is likely that these explanations will have the advantage of making precise and unambiguous the meaning of the questions themselves—which have been set forth in varying ways.

The difficulties which the Congregation for the Doctrine of the Faith sets before you will be a source of pain to you, and the Congregation realizes this. Please accept them, Reverend Father, in a spirit of faith. With the help of the Lord for whom you have done your writing, may they elicit from you a response which leads to or prepares for a satisfactory outcome.

The Congregation for the Doctrine of the Faith is ready to change its interpretations and approaches as circumstances dictate; it has no doubt that you cultivate similar dispositions.

As all of us look forward to a greater or clearer unanimity in our understanding of the faith, our union in prayer to Christ can and must remain unflawed.

(signed) *Franjo Cardinal Seper*
Prefect

SCHILLEBEECKX TO CONGREGATION OF FAITH

April 13, 1977

Introduction

In the letter that accompanied his answer to Cardinal Seper, Schillebeeckx thanked the cardinal for his "Word in Conclusion" at the end of the questionnaire. "I shall try to answer you in all sincerity, realizing as I do that as a theologian I have a limited but real responsibility for the faith; and, refusing to let myself be embittered, I shall answer with great frankness, because I feel myself obliged thereto in conscience." In conversation Schillebeeckx is always inclined to relax tensions rather than to stimulate them; he gives an impression of being irenic. This is much less so when he puts his thoughts on paper. Here his concern is evidently with the issue itself, and he can be seen at times making an effort to dismantle a contrary position down to its last recesses. Anyone who does not know him personally may then be inclined to think that he is rather bent on having his own way. Rather, it is proof that he takes his opponent seriously.

Something of this can be seen in the following response. Especially on sensitive points Schillebeeckx does not mince matters. He points inexorably to errors of translation, inconsistencies, inaccurate linking of ideas, or statements taken out of context in criticisms of his book. On the other hand, he does not go explicitly into all the questions raised; a good many of these, he thinks, are due in large measure to a mistaken idea of the perspective from which he is writing. This is why he allots a good deal of space to introductory reflections in which he establishes the correct perspective. At times, too, one suspects that he simply cannot bring himself to fight what he as a theologian must feel is a rear-guard action. Had not the first session of Vatican II shown the theological approach of his examiners to be unrealistic and unjustified, at least in its claim to universal validity?

The response was in any case written quickly; there was no rough copy, as the author remembers it. He excused himself to Seper for mistakes in his French, which the confidential nature of the matter had prevented him from having reviewed by someone else. There was, even on his part, no thought of publication as he wrote down his thoughts; nor has the text been "corrected" for inclusion in this edition. This is true even of the passage in which he writes: "First of all, a point of detail," without following it out (III/A-2); or his inaccurate page-reference to a passage on the words of institution (II/C), an inaccuracy that was to have (tragi)comic consequences.

After the "preliminary response" on the basic issue—a response that occupies a third of the text—Schillebeeckx makes his way through the list of questions. Consequently we find here the same structure as in the first document. In itself the "preliminary response" is the most gripping part. Here Schillebeeckx lays his cards on the table: he is a pastorally oriented theologian, and will readily even accept the less attractive term "apologetic." But it must be a *serious* apologetic, calling for the most radical historical investigation in which there is no smuggling in of the data of faith as a *deus ex machina* and in which the student searches perseveringly through the past, even without knowing where it will lead him. He did not intend to write a "Christology." English readers should realize that the word "Christology" did not occur in the original Dutch title of the book— the version examined by the Congregation—which in translation reads: "Jesus: The Story of One Who Is Alive" ("Jezus: Het verhaal van een levende"). In spite of this, the censors have fundamentally mistaken his intention—Schillebeeckx undauntedly contrasts them with his many other reviewers, readers and listeners—because they have been unable to take off their habitual "ontological" spectacles. When they see the words "human person" they cannot help thinking of a heresy that was condemned centuries ago, whereas in fact the author is simply adopting the ordinary language of a "flesh-and-blood human being." When they see "starting point" they think of a dogmatic principle, whereas the author means it in the everyday sense of "the point at which you begin" (Introduction [= preliminary response]). They interpret Schillebeeckx' doubts about the use of the *word* "Abba" as doubts about the reality involved (II/D).

Moreover, we find a clarifying distinction between the "Jesus of history" and the "historical Jesus" (Introduction) and see the author explaining that an historical reduction is not an exegetical reduction (*ibid.*) and that "chronologically later" does not have to mean "added by the Church," much less "changeable" or "unimportant" (II/C). In a quite striking way Schillebeeckx opposes any idealizing of the earliest stage, as though the nucleus of revelation were without qualification expressed therein; on the other hand, one must begin there if one wishes to understand the entire process.

In connection with the interpretation of conciliar texts Schille-beeckx once again makes an effort to show the importance of shifts in language (Introduction). In his view "Chalcedon" is primarily a con-tent; in his opponents' view it is evidently a set of words. On the oth-er hand, he accommodates his interlocutors by using their language and notably, for example, by making it clear that "the offer of Jesus" is equivalent to "objective revelation" (I/C) and that the idea of "in-terpretative response" flows from St. Thomas' principle that a person has access only to what is presented in a way in which he or she can grasp it (I/C). Schillebeeckx is not afraid to admit that his interpreta-tion of the appearances of the risen Jesus is the most hypothetical part of his book, but he also corrects the simplistic idea which the censors seem to have of his conversion-model (II/E). He is able to cite Msgr. Descamps, later one of his examiners in Rome, in order to bring home the point that the issue here is entirely an historical question, not a matter of faith.

But as far as the purpose of his work is concerned, Schillebeeckx sees no real opposition between himself and the Congregation. He too is aware of the danger of "confusing" the faithful (I/C, end; Intro-duction), but he thinks this is to be prevented in a different way, namely, by providing reliable information and intelligible interpreta-tion. He believes, too, that he has seen this approach bear fruit. He also hopes that he has cleared away misunderstandings on the part of the Congregation. His concluding words are no less frank than, in his view, the questionnaire had been: the fact that the questionnaire at least attributes the same purpose to him as to itself is "the only evan-gelical consolation the dossier has afforded me."

THE RESPONSE

Replies of Edward Schillebeeckx, O.P.
to Questionnaire No. 46/66
addressed to him by the Congregation for the Doctrine
of the Faith

Before I answer all the questions on particular points, a preliminary response is necessary, I believe, because I have the clear impression that most of the questions reflect certain presuppositions. (*Note:* References to the questionnaire will be indicated by "Dossier" with a page number; references to my book are indicated by "Book" with a page number.)

As I observed repeatedly in my book, this was conceived as supplying prolegomena which were to be followed by other books. As a matter of fact, the second volume on Jesus will appear in a few weeks' time. My plan calls for a trilogy: (a) In the first volume (of which there is question here) my intention was to find out what strict historical method can recover of Jesus' emergence on the scene of our history during his earthly life in Palestine, and then to retrace as it were the journey (*itinerarium mentis*) of the disciples who met a Jew named Jesus and who after his death reached the point of solemnly professing that he was risen and that he was and is in all truth the Son of God, Second Person of the Blessed Trinity. (b) In the second volume, which is about to appear, I attempt to compose a New Testament Christology, that is, I inquire how Christ is seen in the writings of Paul and John, in the Pastoral and the Catholic Letters, in the Letter to the Hebrews, in the Apocalypse, and so on. This volume is directly concerned with an exegesis of the texts of the New Testament canon and no longer (as in Volume I) with a scientific reconstruction of pre-New Testament Christian traditions. (c) In a third volume (which I have only begun) my aim is to deal in a systematic theologi-

46

cal way with the *ecclesiology* and *pneumatology* that are already implicit in the first two volumes.

The first conclusion to be drawn from this plan is that one cannot expect to find already given in the first volume what will be explicitly treated in the second and, still less, the synthesis to be offered in the third. This is why I call the first volume, which is in dispute here, a first set of soundings. On the other hand, at the end of the first three parts of the first volume I already offer an initial, provisional synthesis (one that is relatively brief in comparison with the volume as a whole), because I was afraid that without this synthesis, however summary, many readers might be left confused by a purely historical analysis which only in the second volume is to be supplemented by a reflection in the light of faith.

All this, then, supplies the background of my first volume. In addition, a year before the publication of my book and after a series of pamphlets on "the real Jesus," the notorious book of the German R. Augstein made its appearance. Thousands of Christians read this book and others like it, and were confused; they were left with the clear impression that the Church had been telling them fables and legends and that historical science had now brought the whole business out into the open. Augstein had supposedly shown that the Christ of history could not support the edifice which the Church is said to have erected on the historical phenomenon that was Jesus. In addition, all the newspapers carried reports on Augstein's book, which acted in turn as a catalyst for a number of other little books on "the real Jesus."

A response was needed, not so much against Augstein as such, but for the sake of all the Christians who have been thrown into confusion regarding matters Christological, less by the theologians than by books of that kind. I have done my best to supply this response. (This is also the reason why the black jacket of the Dutch edition was expressly chosen to suggest a counterpart to the black jacket of Augstein's book.)

My purpose, then, was primarily pastoral or, if you prefer, apologetic (but I do not care for this word very much). I was therefore bound to adopt a strictly and even radically historical method in order to get back to the actions, words and deeds of Jesus that might serve as *signs* to every person of good will: signs that might draw their attention to the disciples' response of faith to the historical phenomenon that is Jesus. My aim, then, in this first volume, is to show that the apostolic faith is not an arbitrary superstructure but rather is called for by the person, message, deeds and death of Jesus himself. I do not mean that I wanted to *prove* the faith itself by an historical analysis (that would be absurd). Rather, as I repeat at least three times (Book, 33, 103, 259), I wanted to show that there are enough historical data (that will stand up to every historical examination) for us to *understand* that and how the apostolic faith itself is as it were the flowering (I usually speak of the "reflection," thus the fruit), at the level of faith, of the Jesus who lived in Palestine. Faith alone, of course, can see in the actions and words of Jesus the divine action of God the Savior, but this implies at least that it should be possible to show what kind of actions and words it was that led the early Church to its tremendous faith that this man was God become man.

Anyone attempting to put such a plan into practice must therefore be an honest historian, in the sense that he can state as historically certain only that which is such according to the strict requirements of historical method. Every acquisition at this level is a gain (as I say frequently in my book). On the other hand, the whole enterprise would be vitiated were one to introduce into this analysis data from faith or the intervention of God or ecclesial dogma, since to do so would already imply an act of faith. The Catholic exegete R. Schnackenburg had already observed on a number of occasions that the time was ripe for putting together everything that can from the strictly historical standpoint be claimed as historically certain about Jesus. Consequently, the objection in the dossier that I show a preference for radical Protestant *exegesis* already shows a complete misunderstanding of the purpose of my first volume. The objection really amounts to a demand that I should have already done in my first volume what in fact I have done only in the second. In the project as I envisaged it a minimum of proven historical data is the best that could be expected and is, in any accounting, better than letting pass as historical what cannot be verified by the historical method. Even this minimum (which is still rather large!) is already enough really to raise in the mind of any unprejudiced person a *religious* question to which, obviously, the only answer is an act of faith or non-faith: the question of the identity of Jesus.

For this reason, nowhere in my book do I say that the *historical* image of Jesus, that is, the image of him which historical science can reconstruct, is the norm and criterion of our faith, as the dossier (23f) blames me for doing. This is the direct opposite of what I am saying. It would, moreover, be the most foolish thing a Catholic or Protestant theologian could say. As a matter of fact, I am especially careful in my book to make a clear distinction between "the Jesus of history" (living in the land of Palestine) and the "historical Jesus" (i.e., the abstract picture which historical science can reconstruct of him). It is the Jesus of history, living in Palestine, who is in my view the norm and criterion; he is the origin and cause of the apostolic faith, the concrete content of which can as it were be *"filled out"* by the Jesus of history and not by the abstract reconstruction which science can make of him. On the other hand, it is possible by means of an historical reconstruction to determine what it was in Jesus himself that led disciples contemporary with him to this apostolic faith. If my intention (in the first volume) had been to offer an exegesis of the New Testament (which I do in the second volume, which therefore uses different methods than those used in the first), the objection that I manifest a preference for the most radical exegetes would have been serious and justified. But anyone who has grasped the purpose of my first volume (which I explain in the book, 17–40) will see that the contrary is the case.

Furthermore, I say that even the Jesus of history (living in Palestine) is not the criterion and norm "in the abstract," because we do not know him except through the Gospels, witnesses of the faith. The starting point of our faith is thus not Jesus as such nor the early Church as such, but the two together: that is, *Jesus,* but insofar as he reaches us through the witness of the first Christians, or the first Christians (the Church), but insofar as their testimony is objectively "filled" with what Jesus said and did and with his person. The entire first part of my book (together with the lengthy introduction) attempts to explain this indissoluble connection between the objective historical appearance of Jesus and his Church. I may add that in this unified whole (Jesus and the New Testament testimonies) the Jesus of history (and not the historical Jesus, that is, the result of a scientific historical investigation) enjoys complete priority over the apostolic faith, which simply reflects to us what Jesus truly was (Book, 21, 50, 46, 57, 481, etc.). I repeated all this in detail when I responded to a Protestant professor, H. Berkhof, in an article entitled *"Fides* quaerens intellectum *historicum"* (*Nederlands Theologisch Tijdschrift* 29 [1975] 332–49). In addition, I say explicitly that the historical investigation in my book is carried on "within an intention of faith" and not as a radical or neutral historian. But such an undertaking must imply that the data of faith cannot play *a part in* the historical investigation as such, for if they did the results of a such an "apologetic" enterprise would be rendered meaningless; the whole undertaking would be paralyzed and neutralized in advance. This is why I prepare my readers in the very Foreword of my book by saying that the way in which I am approaching Christology is rather "unconventional" (Book, v), while adding that my ultimate intention nonetheless is to offer a *Christian* Christology.

This method requires that the starting point (which is not the starting point of a Christological synthesis, as the dossier suggests on page 10, but the starting point of an *historical and scientific investigation,* which is quite a different matter) is the meeting of some Jews with another Jew named Jesus; therefore with a human being, a man, or in other words a human person. No historian begins by supposing that these Jews met God in their fellow religionist! This meeting with a Jew was the first experience the disciples had. But I immediately go on to say (the dossier, 10, fails to point this out) that at the end of the disciples' journey with Jesus it will be made clear whether their first impression was valid or erroneous: at the end it will be made clear what the *identity* of this man really is (Book, 33). The entire book was conceived and written in order to show that the disciples' first impression was only provisional, since in the final analysis *it is no longer possible to say without qualification* that Jesus is a human person pure and simple (667).

The dossier, on the other hand, takes "this starting point" as an ontological datum or affirmation; as a result, it has no end of trouble trying to figure out how I can, ontologically, combine the first statement with the second; but the problem is a false one. In fact, there is nothing to *combine!* There is no question of an ontological statement, but only of two phases or stages in the journey of the disciples: (1) the first meeting and their first impression, and (2) the final impression after the death of Jesus (this final impression takes the form of an act of faith in which Jesus is ultimately identified in an ontological way: as the Son of God). The purpose of my book was in fact grasped by all my readers and, with about four or five exceptions, by more than 133 reviewers of my book in all parts of the world. It was precisely this approach that was felt as beneficial by almost all of my readers. The few exceptions were those who from the outset approached by book as though it were concerned with ontology and so understood nothing in it. With one exception (see below), all the questions in the dossier are inspired by ontological reading of the book, whereas it has to be read as a reconstruction of the journey of the disciples who in their encounter with the man Jesus *ended* with an ontological affirmation of faith: this man truly was and is the Son of God. Obviously, he already was the Son of God even before the encounter, even from his conception, even in a pre-existent state; but the recognition of this fact is already the final act of faith and not the beginning of the journey. And my purpose is to offer our confused Christians an historical *manuduc-*

tio or guidance; I want to trace, in its main outlines, the genesis of the apostolic faith.

For myself, as I exercised this *fides quaerens intellectum historicum*, the premise which admitted of no doubt was the dogma of Chalcedon; otherwise I would not have begun this lengthy and rather laborious work. Yet the entire dossier casts doubt on my faith in that Council. Why? I do not understand it at all. I even say explicitly in my book that for my part "*I have no trouble at all with any of this* [the Council of Chalcedon] . . . it [the dogma of Chalcedon] is *straight gospel*" (Book, 462–63, especially 463). Nowhere in the dossier is this important passage cited. But I add that for their part not a few Christians have difficulty with the horizon of philosophical understanding within which the ideas of "hypostasis, nature and person" are located; since that time these ideas have undergone a considerable change of meaning. Faith does not regularly control changes in the meanings of words (it did so in the period of the great Christological disputes, in the fourth and fifth centuries, but not subsequently). The fact must be admitted that even educated people today no longer use the words "nature" and "person" with the same meaning these had in the time of Chalcedon, even though experts may be able to prove to us by subtle analyses that the core meaning of the ideas have not changed. (Such operations are conducted at a level which does not interest the faithful.) It is precisely the intention of the fourth part of my book to translate the dogma of Chalcedon into the language of the faithful. The dossier even gains the impression now and then that I am *moving toward* the dogma of Chalcedon (dossier, 48); it overlooks, however, the fact that it is this dogma itself which compels me to find a paraphrase that will be intelligible to Christians without them having first to be converted (in order to become or remain believers) to a philosophy or a set of meanings which are alien and unintelligible to them. The authors of the dossier have applied a different reading "grid" to my book, while assuming that this theologian must be following anti-Chalcedonian ideas (which I, too, see in the literature and against which precisely I am reacting). But an author is to be read as he stands (*prout jacet*) and not in terms of a tendency which is utterly alien to me.

These preliminary remarks will make it easier for me to give an answer to almost all the questions in the dossier.

Answers to Specific Questions

A. Historical Method

1. Preference for the most radical tendencies in exegesis.—I categorically deny an *exegetical* preference in which I "draw inspiration from the radical wing of Protestant scholarship" (Dossier, 20f). Volume II will be a complete rejection of such a preference. It is true that in Volume I I was obliged to follow the most uncompromising historico-critical method in order that I might establish a firm historical foundation. Otherwise my book would have been without meaning. In this first volume I do not offer an *exegesis* of the New Testament tests (that is the subject of Volume II), but I attempt rather to use these texts as a way of getting back to pre-New Testament traditions.

2. Exegetical reduction.—Historical science as such is reductive by reason of its method; that is why it is, as such, unable to lead us to faith. It is, however, able to reconstruct the historical ground on which pre-New Testament Christians discerned and believed in the saving action of God. This scientific reconstruction enables us to some extent to see that the apostolic faith is not a *superstructure* but the response of faith to the question that is raised by the historical phenomenon called Jesus. Such an historical reduction has nothing to do, either directly or indirectly, with a theological reduction (except possibly for a non-believer; certainly not for me, motivated by *"fides* quaerens intellectum *historicum"*). On the other hand, were one to use a non-historical method (for example, faith) and read too much into the historical data, one would undermine the entire pastoral purpose of supplying a *manuductio* to faith.

3. Premature hermeneutic.—The objection would be valid only if in fact I had undertaken a hermeneutical exegesis of the New Tes-

tament faith (which I do only in Volume II). The area of my work in the first volume was the traditions behind the New Testament and thus the genesis of early Christianity, nothing more.

(a) Nowhere in my book do I say that I view Christ solely in functional terms, as the dossier blames me for doing. Rather I say, consistently with my purpose, that only through what Jesus did and said and suffered (his death), or, in other words, through his functions, is it possible to enter into his person and his identity, which are revealed in and through his functions, at least if one examines these with the eyes of faith. I refuse (as does H. Schlier, for example) to choose between a theology of substance and a theology of function; in any case, this is a modern distinction, unknown to Late Antiquity.

(b) The dossier overlooks the fact that as I see it the eschatological prophet is *messianic;* in my view, the title "eschatological prophet" is not *minimalist* (as the dossier erroneously presupposes), but is rather one of the most maximalist among all the titles to be found in pre-New Testament currents of thought, because it connotes the *universal* importance, value and "relevance" of Jesus for the whole of human history (as I explain even more fully and with more extensive historical documentation in my second volume). Consequently, the second fundamental impression the disciples had of Jesus finds expression in their confession of him as the *messianic* eschatological prophet, the new and infinitely greater Moses. When I say in a particular context that Christ is not Messiah, my meaning is clearly that Jesus rejected the militaristic and nationalistic royal messianism of certain Jewish groups. But there was also a royal messianism that identified the Messiah with the eschatological prophet (as has now been proved in half a score of studies of Johannine thought, as I have shown in Volume II).

Furthermore, in my analysis I am looking for the *initial* Christian expression of faith that is already pregnant with the final expression of that same faith. And with regard to this first expression I warn my readers that "the first articulation of an experience of recognizing [*erkenning*]-and-recollecting [*herkenning*] is not *ipso facto* the richest or more subtle one" (Book, 54). On the other hand, to trace the development of dogma (not only after the close of the New Testament but also) after the death of Jesus down to the final book of the New Testament is already an important exercise of the "intellectus fidei." That is what I have tried to do. There is therefore no premature hermeneutic, but rather a hermeneutic of *one* very early stage in the development of the faith into the apostolic faith of the New Testament.

I am also rebuked for identifying "the cause of God" with "the cause of human beings" (which is in fact a tendency to be found in certain kinds of literature, but certainly not in my book). The dossier forgets to say that for me the contrary takes priority, namely, that "the cause of human beings" is the cause of God, or, in other words, that the salvation of human beings is God himself who for his part wills their salvation (as I have just explained at length in my second volume). I am made to say things which in fact I nowhere say.

B. Jesus of Nazareth as norm and criterion of all interpretation

The heading could not be bettered. But "Jesus of Nazareth" is the Jesus of history and not the "historical Jesus," the figure reconstructed by historical science (Book, especially 67–70)—a central and essential distinction. My position is that the Jesus of history, living in Palestine, is the source and cause, the norm and criterion, the objective determinant of the apostolic faith. I add only that this is why a scrupulous historical reconstruction *can help us to understand* how the apostolic faith was in fact controlled by the objective historical appearance of Jesus. Such is the whole tenor of my book, and I made the point again later on in an article in *Kultuurleven* (42 [1975] 81–93) in which I introduced the book to readers. I deny, therefore, that it is possible to find in my book the following statement which would be such an outlandish one for a Christian to make: "In the final analysis, then, the norm and criterion of any interpretation of Jesus is the Jesus of whom we have historical knowledge" (Dossier, 24–25). I do not understand how the dossier can make such a statement after reading 52–57 of my book; cf. also Book, 44–45.

C. The "offer" of Jesus and "interpretative responses"

For me and the dossier alike this matter is of very great importance. But I fear that the two of us are using the same words to mean different things. I am using this terminology to say what St. Thomas says, namely, that objective revelation becomes revelation in the formal sense by way of the *auditus fidei* [the hearing of faith] and the *assensus fidei* [the assent of faith]. A revelation not heard is an unknown X. "Offer," as I use it, is another word for what is "objectively revealed" in Christ. This is why I do not say simply "offer" (*aanbod*) but always "offer of reality" (*werkelijkheidsaanbod*), that is, the *objective reality* which is given to human beings in Jesus (German translation:

"Angebot der Wirklichkeit," ed. 4, 41; Italian translation: "l'offerta di realtà, Gesù di Nazareth," 42; Dutch edition, 39–40, and English, 48–50). This offer consists in what Jesus says and what Jesus does ("does" includes *agit et patitur*, "does and suffers," and thus includes his death) and, in the final analysis, his very person (whose identity the book is seeking to find by following the journey of the disciples).

To say that a response which articulates the faith is always *interpretative* is simply to restate the epistemology of St. Thomas himself (his principle is that what is received "is received according to the condition of the recipient [*ad modum recipientis recipitur*]"; I explain this in, for example, Book, 48–50). But I have the impression that the dossier identifies my phrase "interpretative faith" (i.e., the articulation of the faith; cf. the medieval "articulus fidei") with a learned German term used by W. Marxsen ("Interpretament"), although in fact I explicitly challenge this ("Explanation of some technical terms," 746; and in greater detail in my article, already cited, in *Nederlands Theologisch Tijdschrift* 29 [1975], especially 333–34). Consequently, when I say that the response of faith is always interpretative, I mean that revelation or, let us say, the word of God comes to us in the shape of human language—in this case, language derived from the Jewish religious tradition. But let me add a qualification: the content of these Jewish key words (Son of man, Son of God, Messiah, the Holy One of God, eschatological prophet, and so on) is "transformed, regauged or corrected" under the impact of the historical appearance of Jesus, that is, of the reality which is Christ (Book, 21). Therefore (as I have just shown in over fifty pages of Volume II), the term "interpretation" does not at all mean a further *arbitrary and subjective* interpretation but rather the very expression of the revealed content in a particular historical context.

But let me give an example. The dossier (27) cites pages 576–79 of my book where I make use of a somewhat subtle distinction from contemporary cultural anthropology, namely, the distinction between three kinds of change: (a) quick and ephemeral developments; (b) long-term changes (which B. Welte and K. Rahner, for example, speak of as "epochale Denkmodellen [models of thinking that persist through long periods]"); and (c) changes which take place over millennia and are hardly detectable. But the dossier makes a fundamental mistake (which explains a lot of things to me) when it *connects* these anthropological distinctions with another distinction which I make in an entirely different context. I am referring to a *linguistic* distinction (which possesses no ontological value) between "first-order assertions" and "second-order assertions." This second distinction (Book,

549) has nothing to do with the other threefold distinction that applies to historical developments. The linguistic distinction, as everyone knows, has nothing to do with the idea of change or development (primary or secondary) but is concerned with the structure of our discourse or spoken language. When a statement refers directly to a reality, linguists call it a first-order assertion; when it refers directly to another statement, they call it a second-order assertion. The distinction thus does not imply that "second-order" means "secondary" in the sense of derivative or "of secondary value," as the dossier supposes. A statement which from a linguistic standpoint is of the second order may even have greater ontological density and value than a first-order assertion. Therefore, the *historical* statement (yet another level!) that (for example) the early Christians initially looked upon Jesus as the eschatological prophet (this assertion is simply a matter of historical investigation) is a first-order assertion. On the other hand, when these same Christians (or a subsequent generation) later say that Jesus is the Son of God made man, they are making a second-order assertion. Yet this second-order assertion has a denser reality, for it develops what is still only implicit in the first assertion. The dossier finds fault with me for saying the exact opposite of what my entire book is saying (cf. especially Book, 549). A second-order assertion is therefore merely more reflexive (this is why I say, although this takes us into the psychological order, that a person who really believes in Jesus as definitive or eschatological salvation from God already implicitly believes all the Christological dogmas, all of which are efforts to render explicit the implications of that first-order assertion).

For this reason I cannot understand what is said in the dossier, page 27, paragraph 2: "This is meant as clarification. . . ." What is being said there has nothing to do with my book. The conclusions are erroneous because the premises are neither mine nor those of my book. For me, first-order assertions are pregnant with all subsequent explicitations of them. Every time I say that this or that statement belongs to a later chronological stage, the dossier almost systematically interprets me as saying that the statement is "therefore superfluous," "therefore of lesser value" or, what is even worse, "therefore changeable." What basis can such an interpretation possibly have in my book? Perhaps one reason for this erroneous interpretation is my use of the expression "overschildering door de kerk," which literally means a repainting, a touching up of an original painting by the Church. The phrase is clearly a metaphor or image intended to "translate" into more vivid terms the rather ponderous phrase: the reactualization or faithful interpretation, in different circumstances,

of what Jesus had said. In Scholastic parlance we might speak of the
"application" of what Jesus had said to new circumstances. The dossier reads into my *overschildering door de kerk* a certain relativism, a
"superposition" that is solely the work of the Church, without objective basis in Jesus himself. But this in no way represents the meaning
of my book. Once again, the dossier has not understood my purpose,
which is to repeat with my readers the journey of the disciples as they
passed from stage to stage to the final emergence of a profession of
faith in the divinity of Christ. It is precisely because they had the
courage to make this journey by means of a difficult and fatiguing but
ultimately rewarding process of analysis that many of my readers
have said as they finished the book: "Yes, it is true." These readers
have retraced the same route, the road as it were from Emmaus to the
point when they could say (or in many instances say once again):
"Yes, it is so. I confess that Jesus is the Christ, the Son of God." We
find the very opposite to be the case in the kind of (rarely theological)
contemporary literature that reduces Jesus to a kind of prophet who
preached only a humanistic social revolution. My book moves entirely in the opposite direction!

Obviously, historians can tell me (at least if they have historical
arguments to offer) that here or there I have fallen into error regarding history, or that this or that is not as historically certain as I claim
it to be. I am the first to admit their right to do so, and in the Foreword of my book (5) I ask them to make such criticisms. I have already received some criticisms of details, and I accept them. But over
forty professional historians and exegetes from many countries have
written to me (or have said in their reviews) that the basic, overall
tenor of my book is difficult to fault. In addition, a dozen or so books
and articles on the Johannine and pre-Johannine traditions that have
since appeared have one after another confirmed my thesis about the
messianic eschatological prophet.

In the context of the triple distinction I make in the book, I must
call attention also to what the dossier says on page 28 (referring to my
book, 581f): "Christology and Trinity, redemption, grace ... it all
seems no longer what we all used to take for granted" (the italics are
mine). These remarks are made in the context not of the linguistic
distinction but in that of the threefold cultural distinction, that is, in
the context of the *epochale Denkmodellen*. People use other *models* in
giving expression to these dogmas; to the person who is not fore-
warned all these truths may *seem* now to be different, but when he
becomes aware of the new model he realizes that in fact the same
truths are being expressed (this is not to imply that every model is ad-

equate). That is what my book is saying and that is how it is normally interpreted. It was to make this point that I wrote pages 576–79 of the book. It is these same distinctions that set the minds of the faithful at ease instead of confusing them and that enable them once again to believe in Jesus Christ as true God and true man (except, I must admit, for Christians of the "Bishop Lefebvre" type).

SECTION II.

A. "A starting point: Jesus as a human person"

I have already explained that this starting point is not for a Christology but for an historical investigation, which is never capable of turning up a God made man. The entire ontological attempt which the dossier makes to harmonize and integrate what is said in Part I of my book with what is said in Part IV is not to the point. There is no need of integrating anything. All that is required is to follow the path from a beginning (first, vague, undefined impression) to the end (final impression, given expression in a profession of faith). Only at the end is the identification of Jesus accomplished; it is at this point that the ontological problem arises for us: How can a human being be the true Son of God? My book *maps out* the steps leading to the blossoming of a God-centered faith, but the dossier misreads it because at every point it can see only metaphysical statements and an exercise in ontology.

Part IV of my book, which offers a provisional synthesis, is in fact located at the level of the ontological identification of the person of Jesus. But at this level I never speak of the human person of Jesus but only of Jesus as "personally human." The dossier adds "sic," showing that the expression is an unusual one, but without asking why the expression is used. Furthermore, the translation in the dossier is incorrect. The dossier translates [literally]: "This man . . . within the confines of a personal-human (French: "personnelle-humaine [sic]") mode of being" (45), whereas the translation should read: "a personal*ly* human mode of being" (French: "personnelle*ment* humaine"). The German translation is correct: ". . . einer personal-menschlichen Seinsweise" (592), whereas the Italian makes the same mistake as the French: "modo di essere personale-umano" (707). [This also applies to the English construction "personal-cum-human" (p. 667)—Ed.] What I am saying, then, is that the mode of being a man is *personalist*—nothing more. Only once do I use the term "human person" in this ontological context, but my purpose then is precisely *to deny* that Christ can be called a human person (Book, 667)! My purpose in speaking as I do is to safeguard the understanding of Christ that is proper to Chalcedon while at the same time doing justice to the modern idea of him. For most modern readers the term "human person" has an entirely different meaning than it had for the councils and the Scholastics. Must these modern readers first be converted to a particular philosophy before they can then be led to the apostolic faith? Of course not. The alternative, then, is to explain Chalcedon to them in their own language. Well, then, for most of our readers a concrete man with an "anima spiritualis," that is, a soul which is formally spiritual and possesses a human intellect, will and love, is a "human person." I myself do not use this term, but say always that Jesus is "personally human"—which is quite a different matter. This is the only way of saving even the terminology of Chalcedon, namely, to say that the humanity of Jesus is personalist, formally spiritual. This is a terminology which even a neo-Chalcedonian could accept. Chalcedon itself does not speak of an an-hypostasis (this is a neo-Chalcedonian term, as Msgr. L. Lebon and Msgr. C. Moeller have clearly demonstrated), but only of an "unus et idem" (one and the same) who is both true God and true man. That is identically the point of view I take throughout the book. But at the same time I take into account the ideas used by my readers. For them, a concrete, formally spiritual human nature is a human person. I myself find this use of "human person" incorrect, and therefore I speak not of "human person" but of "personally human" when I want to indicate that the concrete humanity of Jesus is personalist, formally spiritual, and suffers no lack (because our modern readers are on the alert here; they wait for a writer to deny that anything human is lacking in Christ). Most of my reviewers have grasped what I was doing; in some cases (unfortunately) they even regret that my Christology is still traditional, conservative and Chalcedonian!

These remarks also supply an answer to the question about enhypostasis and anhypostasis (Dossier, 33 and 45–48). I deny only that there was any human lack in the humanity of Jesus (something that St. Thomas, for example, also denies). But, judging by my experience, our view that "another" person can render a "human nature" personal is no longer intelligible to most of our readers. How, then, are we to make the dogma intelligible to them? My solution is the idea of hypostatic identification, that is, not a union of two persons, one human and one divine, but an identification (which is ontological, of course) of the second Person of the Trinity with a formally spiritual human nature. In my judgment, this restates the traditional "hypostatic union" in its purest form. And when the hypostatic union has been explained in this way all my readers have understood and accepted it. (In Germany, Belgium and Holland I have given over twenty lectures on my book to almost ten thousand people, many of whom had already studied it, and my explanation of the hypostatic union was completely satisfactory to them, whereas whenever I said that the divine person functions as person for a human nature, they did not know what I was talking about.) When I said that a divine person *identified himself* with a complete human nature (body and soul), they could understand. Then I would add: That is precisely the dogma of Chalcedon. Consequently, almost all my readers, unless prejudiced, would rightly challenge the dossier in its suspicion that I am in favor of "the project of a host of contemporary theologians" (Dossier, 34).

B. "Jesus . . . not *as Messiah* but *as eschatological prophet*"

This opposition between "not" and "but" is nowhere to be found in my book and is indeed contrary to the book's basic intention. As seen in the book, the eschatological prophet is not the precursor of the Messiah (as he was in some Jewish currents of thought) but the Messiah himself. He is the messianic eschatological prophet (cf., e.g., Book, 477). In my second volume I have just given more extensive historical documentation and explained that the eschatological prophet is kingly, priestly, and messianic—in short, the Mosaic Messiah.

Furthermore, I do not leave a gap (as the dossier does, 36) between what Jesus thought and what the disciples made of him. The whole purpose of my book is to show that what the disciples say of Jesus after his death is the reflection, the articulative and fully conscious unfolding of what Jesus himself in fact was and said. I deny absolutely, therefore, that there is any question in my book of "the absence of any messianic project on the part of Jesus" (Dossier, 36).

C. Jesus, Servant of Yahweh, handed over for our sins

As a matter of fact, this statement represents in my eyes the climax of what I was trying to say in the book. Yet in the dossier the statement is turned into an objection against me.

Where in my book do I deny that "the words of eucharistic institution" (Dossier, 37) have their basis in the history of Jesus? I rally, says the dossier, to the views of W. Marxsen! But in this whole context the only reference I make is to the Catholic exegete H. Schürmann (cf. the notes of the book, 699). With him I make a distinction between two textual strata in the New Testament: (a) texts already showing liturgical formulation (and therefore presupposing the liturgical life of the early Church), and (b) an older stratum, which I say, with F. Hahn, belongs "zum Urgestein des Traditionstückes" ("to the primeval rock of the tradition," Book, 308). The dossier insinuates that *therefore* I deny the institution of the Eucharist by Christ. The authors seem to be reading W. Marxsen's book rather than mine. I expressly say that these eucharistic texts *faithfully represent* the *historical* actions and words of Christ (Book, 308).

I admit that I say nothing, at least directly, about a sacrificial soteriology (Dossier, 38). The dossier's claim is almost true. True: because a sacrificial soteriology is the theme of my second volume (as I twice say in so many words in Volume I, 35 and 669). *Almost* true (and to this extent not true): because, looking forward to Volume II, I say explicitly that in the final analysis Jesus of Nazareth accepted his death as part of his salvific purpose (Book, 310–11 and 542–43). The implications of all this, including the ideas of sacrifice, satisfaction, and so on, are developed at length in Volume II.

D. Jesus and God his Father

I must admit that these pages of the dossier are especially painful to me. In my view, reacting as I do against a purely humanizing tendency that removes the constitutive relationship between Jesus and his father, my pages on God as the Abba of Jesus Christ are the very heart of my entire book. Why then—the answer is beyond me—does the dossier link these pages with a nineteenth century Protestant thesis? It is precisely this unique, conscious relationship of Jesus to his father that provides me with a way of affirming the hypostatic union (my article in *Nederlands Theologisch Tijdschrift* 29 [1975] 345–46, is even more explicit). The dossier minimizes everything I said in this chapter by taking as the basis for its explanation my statement that the *word* Abba as such settles nothing. (Once again, the writers of the dossier forget the requirements of rigorous historical investigation.) In my view, it is not the word Abba as such that explains the unique relationship of Jesus with his Father (*even* if the word was never used by contemporary Jews), but rather this almost unique word as used in the total context provided by the person, preaching and practice of Jesus (Book, 259–69). This contextual use is what is decisive, and this is my position as formulated in the dossier (41; where, however, it becomes an objection against me). The very text of the dossier seems doubtful anyway of its own interpretation of my book (Dossier, 41), in the paragraph beginning, "Are you not worried. . . ."

I grant that disagreement is possible (Dossier, 42) on the statement that Jesus "never posited himself (beside the rule of God) as the *second* object of his preaching" (Book, 258; although I think the statement is justified at the historical level). But I deny the conclusion the dossier draws from the statement. For the Gospels (and for me) the Kingdom of God is Jesus. I deny only that this is the primary affirmation made at the very outset (and my intention is to trace the course of the successive affirmations made by the disciples). In fact, I frequently call attention to the early tradition known as Q, in which it is said that to opt for or against the Kingdom of God is to opt for or against Jesus (I add that these words are very likely authentic words of Jesus). In these words there is an implicit identification between Kingdom and Jesus, and this on the lips of Jesus himself. The explicit identification (found especially in the Johannine tradition) is therefore simply a legitimate explicitation of Jesus' self-awareness, and this is precisely what the book aims to show! But the authors of the dossier seem to forget that the book's purpose is to trace the development of pre-New Testament dogma.

E. Easter as a turning point

I am very grateful to see in the dossier an admission that I profess "the personal and bodily resurrection of Jesus" (two reviewers find in my book a denial of this very point).

The difficulties the dossier raises have to do with my explanation of the appearances. I admit it: this point is (I do not say the weakest but) scientifically the most hypothetical in the book. But before giving my answer I may mention one of my expert reviewers, Msgr. Descamps of Louvain (and I might add Msgr. A. Prignon). Msgr. Descamps raises exegetical difficulties against my explanation, but he explicitly adds that whatever the value of the interpretation it remains entirely within the confines of Catholic orthodoxy. In short, the question is a purely historical one, at least if one acknowledges in them (as I do) a divine revelation of the resurrection of Christ. I accept *that which*, in the story of the appearances, is the intention of the narrative, namely, to say that the event is a pure favor from God, given in and through Christ who after his death lives on with the Father and that consequently the profession of the bodily resurrection of Jesus is not the result "of flesh and blood" but of a divine revelation. This is the core of the dogma.

I also acknowledge (in the short popular book cited by the dossier, 44) that from an historical standpoint there is no room for rejecting even the visual elements in the Easter event. The main point of my argument is simply to deny that these visual elements are the *foundation* of our faith in the resurrection (the fact that sermons often take such an approach is something that offends many of the faithful and casts ridicule on the dogma). Furthermore, I ask, as an historian, what the particular events were which are accessible to a historian and through which this divine revelation presented itself. I do not deny a priori that a real appearance may have been the medium for this divine revelation. I say only that there were conversion models presented in the form of appearances and that I see such models at work in the biblical account of the appearances. It is obviously possible to ask whether or not my interpretation is plausible from an exegetical standpoint. It is on this point above all that I gladly await exegetical arguments which may invalidate my exegesis. Thus far these arguments have not been forthcoming (some reviewers simply reject my position but offer no arguments against it).

But even if a reader is not in agreement with my interpretation, he has an obligation to distinguish honestly between what I say and what I do not say: (a) I deny (contrary, once again, to W. Marxsen) that faith in the resurrection is nothing but a post-paschal *interpretation* of the pre-paschal life of Jesus (Book, 393–94). Precisely because an overhasty reading led some to interpret my book in that fashion I introduced into the third Dutch edition of my book (first edition of all the translations) five pages in which I repeat my reaction against Bultmann, W. Marxsen and others (Dutch, 528a-e [English, 644–50]).—(b) I do not deny the psychological (and therefore historical) realities involved (Dossier, 43). On the contrary, I seek to figure out what happened historically, so as to free our preaching from the kind of hocus-pocus often found in sermons on these matters. I say that the intention of the appearance reports is to supply "a specific, foundational testimony" (as the dossier rightly puts it, 44). My words are:

"The New Testament suggests an undeniably intrinsic connection between Jesus' resurrection and the Christian, faith-inspired experiences at Easter, expressed in the model of 'appearances' " (Book, 645). In addition: "It is evident from that analysis of the Easter experience that the objective cannot be separated from the subjective aspect of the apostolic belief in the resurrection" (Book, 645), and that "without being identical with it, the resurrection of Jesus—that is, what happened to him, personally, after his death—is inseparable from the Easter experience, or faith-motivated experience . . . the work of the Spirit of Christ" (*ibid.*).—(c) I also say (though in different words) that the Easter experience of the apostles "ended" "by right and in fact" (as the dossier legitimately puts it, 44; cf. my book, 646–47), but I add that all Christians must have an *analogous* Easter experience: a renewal of life, based on the resurrection.—(d) I stress the point that this "conversion" of the apostles is not just any *metanoia* whatsoever (of the kind that are the law of Christian life) but rather "the major transformation" by reason of which, after the death of Christ and as a result of new occurrences of grace, "the disciples acknowledge and confess him as the Christ" (Book, 645). This conversion was thus a real *Christophany*—and that is precisely the meaning of the appearances. Perhaps my use of the word "conversion" both in a moral and, above all, in a Christological sense is confusing. In any case, when I use this terminology of conversion the essential element in it is the Christophany, just as it is in the terminology of the appearances: *ōpthē* ("he was seen"). It is the living Christ, the risen one, who opens their eyes (the *cognitive* element in these post-Easter experiences).

My statement that the New Testament text "Where two or three are gathered in my name, there am I in the midst of them" is "perhaps the purest, most adequate expression of the Easter experience" (Book, 646) is taken out of context in the dossier 44, although I admit that my words may be ambiguous. I cite this biblical text in order to bring out the intrinsic connection between the resurrection, as an event involving Christ, and his glorified heavenly presence in his Church (this is the context for my statement, which is not meant as an expression of the Easter experience itself). Without the resurrection there is no presence of Christ in his Church (these pages were written in reaction to W. Marxsen).

SECTION III

A. Incarnation and Trinity

1. On page 19 the dossier congratulates me because in my book I reach the point of "recognizing in God the Trinitarian fullness that is made up of the Father, the Son who appeared in Jesus, and the Spirit who animates the Church" (as if this recognition were something surprising in a theologian who desires to be a Catholic). But pages 45–49 of the dossier seem to suggest the contrary. I have already explained my position (above, Section II). This explanation makes it clear that all the abstractly possible interpretations offered in the dossier, 45–46, are irrelevant to my book. I simply acknowledge, after rereading the entire context, that my formula "mutual *en*hypostasis" may in fact be ambiguous, especially to Scholastic minds. My purpose in using this terminology is to make intelligible what the Greek Fathers mean when they speak of perichoresis and theandrism, namely, that the person of the Logos envelops the entire personalist (= formally spiritual) humanity of Jesus and that this concrete humanity does not remain extrinsic to or outside of the hypostasis of the Logos. The dossier itself (48) is compelled to acknowledge that many of my pages give reason to "hope for a rediscovery of Chalcedon." Well, as far as I am concerned, Chalcedon is the norm that governs all of my theological studies; it is to this dogma that I wish to "lead by the hand" (*manuducere*) the Christians of our day who have their fill of books about the "death of God" and about Jesus being only a man, though a great prophet. If I regarded Chalcedon as a dead letter, I would not have the courage or the desire to write two books on Jesus which together come to over fourteen hundred pages.

2. *The Most Blessed Trinity.*—First of all, a point of detail. The dossier evidences a misconception about the citation: "God would be no God without creatures and Jesus of Nazareth" (Book, 668; Dossier, 48). The wording is admittedly somewhat unusual, but it must be seen in context. I am a disciple of St. Thomas and therefore find any idea of emanation absurd. Creation and the incarnation are free acts of God. But God's freedom is not a *contingent* "liberum arbitrium" [power of free choice]. Contingency marks the effects of God's action but not the divine action itself which is identical with the divine essence, as Aquinas says. It would be entirely false to say that "God would be no God without creatures . . ." if the statement were taken *ex parte Dei* [from the side of God] but not if it is taken *ex parte creatur-*

arum [from the side of creatures]; in other words, *given* the contingent fact of the existence of creatures and of Jesus, God is essentially a Creator God and eternally the origin of the incarnation, but he is these by a divinely free act. This is the very principle of divine immutability.

B. *Virginal conception of Jesus*

On this point the dossier has not failed to grasp the meaning of what I say; it does, however, forget that in my book I say nothing either for or against this profoundly authentic addition of the Church. In this first volume I have only studied the meaning of the virginal conception in Matthew and Luke (and in my exegesis I have chiefly followed Catholic exegetes). These exegetes note that in the Church of the New Testament there were several currents of thought on this subject. One of these could not explain the divinity of Christ except by means of a virginal conception; there are other New Testament currents that do not know of this necessary link. The exegetes also observe a tendency to dissociate the two concepts, with the stress being laid increasingly on the biological aspect of the virginal conception, while its religious significance is forgotten (this is especially the case in the apocrypha).

In my book I do not deal with the virginal conception as such, but only as a factor in the pre-New Testament development of dogma: Jesus acknowledged as the Christ by reason of his resurrection; Jesus acknowledged as already the Christ from the moment of his baptism; Jesus acknowledged as the Christ from his birth; and Jesus acknowledged as the pre-existent Christ. The virginity is not studied as such in this context. No conclusions may be drawn with regard to my personal position, since it is not given in this first volume. I grant, of course, that I must make my own position known in the second or third volume of my trilogy. For I acknowledge that in addition to Sacred Scripture there is also the great Christian tradition. In Volume I I am, in effect, leaving the question open. One might find fault with me on the grounds that a theologian does not have the right to leave certain authentic aspects of the faith temporarily in suspense. In my judgment, the decision to do so depends on circumstances. Since my book is addressed chiefly to those Catholics and other Christians who have difficulties with Christian dogma, I am convinced that the principle of Jesus, "You cannot bear them now" ("non potestis portare modo," Jn 16:12), has a legitimate pastoral application, provided that the silence does not concern the "substantia fidei" ["substance of the faith"] and that it is only temporary.

C. The Church

I speak of the Church constantly throughout my book, but in this first volume I deliberately, though provisionally, use chiefly such terms as "Christian community" or "movement centered on Jesus." (Ecclesiology will be the subject of my third volume; given the pastoral and "apologetic" nature of the three volumes I intend a kind of gradual ascent to the fullness of dogma.) Marginal believers (whose numbers are increasing daily and who are not the worst around) will not be brought to Christ by our repeating the word "Church" as a sacred talisman; quite the contrary! Our task is to lead them without scaring them off in advance by a terminology which in their eyes is already loaded down with all the sins of Israel.

On several official occasions—during lectures—I myself expressed dissatisfaction with the interview to which reference is made in the dossier, 51. In addition, the French translation of the text of the interview is out-and-out inaccurate. The dossier wrongly has "sense of union" [as translation of "verbondenheid" with the Vatican] whereas I in fact say that my sense of union with Rome remains intact but that ever since the Council the *affective* element (in this sense of union) is weakened or missing among theologians. These are two quite different things! (And some of the Roman Congregations are aware of what some theologians associated with *Concilium* have done to improve this de facto situation.) But even if my intention was not faithfully conveyed in the interview, I very much doubt that the text would dismay the faithful.

Such, then, are my initial answers. I think and hope that they have cleared up a number of misunderstandings. Like the dossier, I have spoken frankly, with the good of the Church in mind. Like the dossier, I am convinced that there are abroad in the churches Christological tendencies which depart from the great Christian tradition. Like the dossier, I fight these tendencies. There is, it seems, a difference in methods between the dossier and my book as we go about combatting this infidelity. But our goal, as I see it, is the same. This is the only evangelical consolation the dossier has afforded me.

CONGREGATION
OF FAITH
TO SCHILLEBEECKX

July 6, 1978

Introduction

It is not easy to define the literary genre of the third document, which was sent to Schillebeeckx on July 6, 1978, along with an invitation to a conversation in Rome. In the letter which accompanied the document Cardinal Seper explained that Schillebeeckx' answers had supplied "some helps to clarification" but "had not succeeded in elucidating completely the basic questions posed to him" and therefore "could only be regarded" by the Congregation "as insufficient." To this letter was attached an "evaluation" of Schillebeeckx' answers by "one of our experts."

Apart from such an identification this extensive document is anonymous and, unlike the initial "questionnaire," does not carry the seal of the Congregation. As was said before: it reminds one to some extent of a scholarly discussion in a traditional Scholastic periodical, complete with footnotes, references to further literature, and arguments of a kind that make the head swim. On the other hand, the introduction leads one to expect that a kind of impartial balance sheet will be drawn up of the differences between the viewpoints of the first two documents, with a careful mention of the points on which Schillebeeckx was correct, "even on small details." But, of course, the document is not quite neutral; the "evaluation" frequently turns into an indictment. Oddly enough, the anonymous author speaks often in the first person, but when it becomes somewhat more difficult or embarrassing, he does not hesitate to speak in the name of "the Congregation" and even of "the Church" (in his view, indeed, the two terms probably amount to the same thing). Clearly, no written answer is expected from the accused; the document is meant to let him see what he must answer to during the "conversation" in Rome.

The structure of the document, however, is not determined by the nine points listed in the accompanying letter as topics for the conversation. The greatest part of this document deals with the Christological problem, without making any clear distinction (as the first document, the questionnaire, had) between questions of methodology, history and systematic theology. From the structural standpoint this document is much weaker than the first. Consider, for example, the odd grouping under a single heading of Jesus' virginal conception and resurrection. Section D, on "Jesus, 'Servant of Yahweh,' " is in fact concerned with the Eucharist.

And yet the composer of this document had had almost a year in which to do his work. He seems to have devoted his energies primarily to gathering new proofs that Schillebeeckx was wrong on points of detail, especially where the latter had been able to point out mistakes or a lack of understanding in the first document. In addition, a contribution of Schillebeeckx to the notorious issue of *Tijdschrift voor Theologie* on Christ (1966, no. 3) is now brought into the picture (had this been the occasion for starting dossier 44/*66*?). The author of the Evaluation frequently catches himself discussing points that do not touch on faith—something that lies outside his commission. Thus, for example, the section on the "empty tomb" at the resurrection of Jesus (H-2), the use of the word "Abba" (E-3), and the royal Messiah, a concept which he must greatly restrict in order to rescue it, and even then only through an appeal to "the harmony of the two Testaments" (C, end).

Another striking trait is that not only are many counter-arguments of Schillebeeckx not taken seriously, but also, and especially, no attention is paid to his lengthy discussion of purpose and method. The factor which is crucial to Schillebeeckx is actually simply ignored, and the result is that the new "questions" (which are often more pointed versions of the original questions) fall outside Schillebeeckx' context and do battle with phantoms. Of course, for Roman theology the context of someone's thinking—and this holds even for definitions of dogma—has never been regarded as very important. The discussion there is of immutable truths which are thought to be independent of the cultural context and language in which they are formulated. Schillebeeckx' attempt (for the umpteenth time) to alter this outlook seems to have been ineffectual (B-4).

The tone of the reply is far from pleasant. The author suggests, among other things, that Schillebeeckx' objection to Spitz's interview is insincere (F-2, e). He says that he, the writer, is *"unfortunately* certain" that Schillebeeckx does not do justice to the faith (F-2) and, in connection with a formulation he calls "obscure," he remarks: "Fortunately (or, rather: unfortunately) the author explains" what he intends (F-2, e). He claims that Schillebeeckx' choice of words gives him an "unearned advantage" (fn. 15), and he sarcastically records "a slight—very slight—concession" on Schillebeeckx' part (F-2, b). Twice in succession he remarks that "Fr. Schillebeeckx begins by congratulating himself" (H-1 and 2; it is unclear whether the writer grasps the irony of Schillebeeckx' statement). We also find the following lovely sentence: "This is odd indeed; for it would have been by contradicting him that the disciples explicitated what Jesus said" (C, near the end),—overlooking, apparently, that the "contradiction" is of his own making. The writer also goes in for understatement: he speaks of "the fear of a certain dogmatic relativism" (B-4) and of Schillebeeckx "allowing [himself] to be *tempted* by a theology of a *more or less* Nestorian kind" (F, end). And the thing I found most bewildering was the writer's excusing himself for engaging in "rather fine-spun" arguments; this, he says, is necessary because Schillebeeckx started it (F-1, end).

This last point is a good occasion for calling attention to a matter of content which the writer introduces with that excuse. The evaluation objects to the phrase "hypostatic identification" which Schillebeeckx uses in order to make the content of the traditional phrase "hypostatic union" intelligible to the modern listener. By a minute analysis of a number of passages in Schillebeeckx, an analysis that is understood, of course, solely from within the writer's own framework, he tries to prove that Schillebeeckx must fail to do justice to Christ's divinity. In the course of this labyrinthine argument we come up against the great danger in this kind of theology with its "clear and firm" language (F-2, e): the theologian unsuspectingly talks in the same manner about, e.g., "divine nature" and "human nature," and thus uses the adjectives "divine" and "human" as though they referred to equal realities, like "human" and "animal." He thus obscures the fact that he is really dealing with two radically unequal realities that cannot be added together; the "divine" ultimately eludes us and can only be approximated in "extrapolated," analogical language. The clarity, therefore, is only illusory.

Here, on the contrary, Schillebeeckx' "faltering" speech is perfectly in place (F-2, near the beginning): a consciousness of the gulf between God and man and therefore a search for words that will suggest and evoke (even) this gulf. In the use of the term "identification" (for example) Schillebeeckx' "apologetic procedure" certainly plays a part; whoever really comes to know Jesus as a man (and during that time Jesus is, for him, just a man), will finally, like the first disciples, feel compelled at last to "identify" him with God. It is not without reason, therefore, that Schillebeeckx speaks of "a kind of hypostatic identification"; this too is symbolic language. This "a kind of" is probably what bothers the censor most; it is completely out of place in his type of theology. Yet even Thomas Aquinas, who could never forget that what we know best about God is what he is *not*," often uses "quodammodo" or "quasi," especially in connection with his own theological discoveries.

In this light it is quite understandable that for years Schillebeeckx has been unwilling to say that Jesus is "God *and* man"—a passage which the evaluator cites (F-2, e), but omitting the emphasis on the "and." This emphasis, which is a "faltering" stylistic device, illustrates, in the final analysis, the great difference between traditional and modern theology. Unfortunately, only the latter is conscious of the difference.

Finally, the reader may well experience some malicious enjoyment at the anonymous writer's vain efforts to track down on page 253 of the Dutch *Jezus* (English, 308) a passage which says, according to Schillebeeckx, that he traces the words of eucharistic institution back to Jesus himself. This time the censor has *not* searched long enough in the book. The sentence is right next to it, on page 252 (English, 307). We will see a vestige of this same mistake in the conversation in Rome.

EVALUATION OF ANSWERS

Evaluation of the Answers
given by Father Schillebeeckx to the questions
of the Congregation for the Doctrine of the Faith
on his book Jesus: An Experiment in Christology

INTRODUCTION

The author has submitted a very detailed reply to the Sacred Congregation for the Doctrine of the Faith (S.C.D.F.). In it he makes almost no concession, but his tone is polite.

My approach here will not be to follow Fr. Schillebeeckx step by step through the reflections he offers in his answers. I shall attempt rather a critical and, above all, a just judgment on a series of important doctrinal questions, while connecting with these other doctrinal questions of lesser importance. If, as I go, it seems to me that on certain points or even on small details the author is in the right as against the questionnaire, I shall be careful to point this out.

I shall deal in order with the following questions: (A) "Jesus of Nazareth, norm and criterion of any interpretation of Jesus" (Book, 43); (B) the Christological interpretations of the Bible, tradition, and systematic theology; (C) the messiahship of Jesus; (D) Jesus the "Servant of Yahweh"; (E) Jesus and his Father; (F) on "hypostatic identification"; (G) the mystery of the Trinity in God; (H) the virginal conception of Jesus and the mystery of his resurrection.

References to Fr. Schillebeeckx' book will be indicated by the letter B; references to the questionnaire, by Q; and references to Fr. Schillebeeckx' responses to the questionnaire, by R.

A. "Jesus of Nazareth, norm and criterion of any interpretation of Jesus"

1. With regard to this title, which is the author's, the S.C.D.F. made two observations. The first is that Jesus of Nazareth can be a "norm and criterion" only to the extent that he is known, and that the author gives his reader to understand that he is referring to Jesus insofar as he can be reached by the historian. Let me explain briefly this twofold observation.

The S.C.D.F. found the author frequently speaking of Jesus himself or his "offer" and of the acceptance of this "offer" as being always a kind of "interpretative response." It went on to note that the author himself acknowledges that Jesus (and his "offer") are known only through a mediation, and that the author explains as follows the title of the section here under consideration: "The starting point for any Christology or Christian interpretation of Jesus is not simply Jesus of Nazareth, still less the Church's *kerygma* or creed. Rather it is the *movement* which Jesus himself started in the first century of our era; more particularly because this Jesus is known to us, historically speaking, only via that movement.... In other words, the starting point is the first Christian community—but as a reflection of what Jesus himself was, said and did" (B 44 [the word "movement" is italicized in the Dutch original.—Tr.]). And again: "What that offer [of salvation] was we can only infer indirectly from the reactions and other evidences recorded in the New Testament" (B 44). After citing these two passages the questionnaire added: "In the final analysis, then, the norm and criterion of any interpretation of Jesus is the Jesus of whom we have historical knowledge" (Q 24–25).

Fr. Schillebeeckx objects strongly to this conclusion. First of all, he says: "The starting point of our faith is ... not Jesus as such nor the early Church, but the two together: that is, *Jesus,* but insofar as he reaches us through the witness of the first Christians, [or: the first Christians (ed.)] (the Church), but insofar as their testimony is objectively 'filled' with what Jesus said and did and with his person.... [There is an] indissoluble connection between the objective historical appearance of Jesus and his Church. I may add that in this unified whole (Jesus and the New Testament testimonies) the Jesus of history (and not the historical Jesus, that is, the result of a scientific historical investigation) enjoys complete priority over the apostolic faith, which simply reflects to us what Jesus truly was" (R 61). In short, if I understand correctly, Jesus himself and the first response to his offer are indissolubly connected, and he has priority over this response, which simply reflects him.

I confess that I do not see how all this prohibits one from saying that, according to Fr. Schillebeeckx, *as far as we are concerned* Jesus is the *criterion* and norm of any theological interpretation to the extent that he is historically known through the writings of the first Christians.

But Fr. Schillebeeckx insists on the point and refers us (R 62) to a passage in his book in which he explicitly says that his historical research is carried on "within an intention of faith." Let us cite the passage: "A (modern) Christological interpretation of Jesus cannot start from the *kerygma* (or dogma) about Jesus, or indeed from a so-called 'purely historical' Jesus of Nazareth; whereas a historical and critical approach, set within an intention of faith, remains the only proper starting point" (B 56). Let us add, therefore, that there is question of an historical knowledge which is not the result of a study lacking in any predisposition (although, to tell the truth, this seems self-evident) and that the predisposition which Fr. Schillebeeckx claims for himself is "an intention of faith."[1] The words of the questionnaire to which Fr. Schillebeeckx objects do not say all of this, but neither do they deny it; moreover, the questionnaire had already acknowledged that Fr. Schillebeeckx had written his book "as a contribution to the expansion of Christ's reign" (Q 19; cf. 18). I do not think that the S.C.D.F. has fallen into any real misunderstanding on the point in dispute here.

2. But, it may be asked, is the question important? Yes, it is, and I shall say why. If the issue here were simply the historical dimension of fundamental theology, it might be said that the norm and criterion of conclusions about Jesus must be Jesus himself insofar as he is accurately reflected (which criticism would have to establish) by the testimonies recorded in the New Testament. But Fr. Schillebeeckx speaks

---

1. The author gives a rather nuanced explanation of this "intention of faith": "In faith, but yet identifying myself with the doubts concerning the 'Christ of the Church,' which . . . I have heard so sharply expressed all around me . . . I have set out to search for 'meta-dogmatic' clues—that is, through and beyond ecclesiastical dogma, although aware that this very dogma had driven me to undertake the search—and to pursue them without knowing in advance where this would take me, without even knowing where this line of attack was not in the end bound to fail" (B 34).

In addition, the author shows an odd preference for the rather radical wing of Protestant critics: such men as K. Berger, a man whose work is much disputed (but Fr. Schillebeeckx is congratulated here by his friend B. van Iersel [*Kosmos & Oekumene* 8 (1974) 177]), Ferd. Hahn, S. Schulz (another author regarding whom there is sharp disagreement. Fr. Schillebeeckx attempts to justify this preference by saying that in his book he is doing critical history, not exegesis (R 66). The answer is a weak one.

of the historically known Jesus as the norm and criterion of *any* interpretation of Jesus. Any *interpretation* of Jesus or any *Christology* (the
author identifies the two, B 44): what does this mean? The reader may
ask whether the writer is staying in the area of fundamental theology
or whether he is moving beyond this into the area of systematic theology, or even—because the word "any" is used—that of biblical and
traditional Christology.

This point, which is extremely important, will be taken up in the
next section.

B. The Christological interpretations of Scripture, tradition, the magisterium and systematic theology

1. *The Christological interpretations of Scripture.*—On the basis of his
historical study of Jesus, the author tirelessly repeats that Jesus presented himself as "the eschatological [supreme, definitive] prophet
from God" (thus B 245) and that faith in its very first form accepted
this "offer" of Jesus. Faith, then, acknowledged Jesus as eschatological prophet and as "salvation in Jesus coming from God" (*Heil-in-Je-
zus van Godswege*). This, says Fr. Schillebeeckx, was the title he
originally intended to give to his book, but it would perhaps have
meant nothing before the book had been read through (B 557).

This "offer" of Jesus and the central, primordial response of faith
form an inseparable whole (B 21, 357–58). The initial and central response of faith directly expresses an experience (B 34–35, 38). Faith is
almost synchronous with this experience. Therefore Fr. Schillebeeckx speaks of (the expression) "definitive salvation-coming-from-
God in Jesus of Nazareth, the crucified-and-risen One" as "the given
factor" (B 655). This "given factor" will be the criterion and norm for
subsequent expressions and, in the first place, for the four interpretations or "Christologies" or "creeds" (B 403) which the author finds to
be the primitive ones in the New Testament.

These creeds confess (1) the "Lord who comes"; (2) the *"theios
anèr"*; (3) Wisdom coming to earth and then returning to heaven; (4)
Jesus crucified and risen. These four creeds are divergent and to some
extent opposed (B 383–84). One of them (the *theios anèr*) is rejected by
St. Paul as a preaching of "another Jesus" (2 Cor 11:4); furthermore, it
does not become canonical. Another creed (confessing Wisdom to
have come down to earth and then returned to heaven) comes from
" 'sophisticated' Graeco-Jewish circles" (B 432). Nonetheless, all of

them (though not without undergoing correction by one another) could contribute to the image of Jesus which the New Testament offers to us (B 439). For, in the final analysis, all of them had for their focus the figure of the eschatological prophet and the basic idea of salvation in Jesus Christ, which is "the basic creed of all Christianity" (B 440); each of them approaches this figure and idea from the standpoint of divergent aspects of ideas current at the time.

After having, in a debatable manner (but this point I leave aside), identified four creeds as unqualifiedly primitive, Fr. Schillebeeckx examines the Christological titles which, he claims, were introduced later on into the Christian community of the first century, namely, "Christ," "Lord," "Son." These he likewise sees as deriving from the disciples' experience of Jesus as definitive messenger of God, as the one in whom salvation comes to us from God. Consequently, if the experience of the "offer" of Jesus found expression in various titles, it did so in function of various currents of thought.

I also take the liberty of citing here a passage from a lecture which Fr. Schillebeeckx recently delivered at Utrecht, for it touches on our subject and offers clarification. Fr. Schillebeeckx says: "We see that one and the same fundamental experience is expressed in very different ways by the different New Testament writers. Although the experience is one, there is a certain tension between it and the interpretation given of it in each New Testament document. . . . But are Christians, then, bound by the 'interpretaments' [a neologism coined, I believe, by W. Marxsen], that is, by the Jewish and Greek elements of interpretation which the New Testament writers used to give a translation of their experience that was conditioned by an age and determined by social and cultural conditions? . . . The Christian, who believes in the saving value of the life and death of Jesus, cannot in addition be obliged to believe all these 'interpretaments' [that are in Scripture and tradition]. Earlier images (*beelden*) and 'interpretaments' of the past can in fact lose their significance (*irrelevant worden*)" (E. Schillebeeckx, in *Kosmos & Oekumene* 11 [1977] 296).

Does not the Jesus whom Fr. Schillebeeckx reaches through history—Jesus the eschatological messenger of God, Jesus in whom salvation-coming-from-God is to be found—seem in fact to be the norm for subsequent expressions of the faith, which are more or less relativized? These subsequent expressions have validity, it seems, to the extent that within certain horizons of understanding (in certain ideological contexts) they are suited to maintaining this response, this primordial experience.

And is this not what the author of *Jesus: An Experiment in Christology* had already given us to understand? Let me cite some further passages. "I believe in Jesus (of Nazareth): the Christ, the only-begotten Son, our Lord; I believe in Jesus as that definitive saving reality which gives final point and purposes to my life" (B 30). And: "I have written this book as a piece of reflective thinking about Jesus of Nazareth, whom the churches of Christ, to which I belong, confess *as final salvation:* in Jewish terms, the Christ, Son of God and son of man; in Hellenistic terms, the Son of God in a fully ontological sense" (B 33 [italics in the Dutch original.—Tr.]).

2. *The Christological interpretations of tradition and the magisterium.*—In his book Fr. Schillebeeckx has but little to say about Christology in the course of the tradition, especially as it found expression in the formulas of Nicea and Chalcedon. The questionnarie which the S.C.D.F. sent him said as much: "You do, of course, think that account should be taken of the teaching of Scripture and the Church when the effort is being made to offer new Christological interpretations; but you do not seem to regard this teaching as providing norms which determine once and for all the meaning of the objects of faith" (Q 25). Is this criticism justified? I shall answer primarily by allowing Fr. Schillebeeckx to speak.

Nicea—"From the Council of Nicea onward," he says, "one particular Christological model—the Johannine—has been developed as a *norm* within very narrow limits and in one direction; and in fact only this tradition has made history (*geschiedenis gemaakt heeft*)[2] in the Christian churches. For that reason the course of history has never done justice to the possibilities inherent in the Synoptic model; its peculiar dynamic was checked and halted (*afgeremd*) and the model relegated to the 'forgotten truths' of Christianity. . . . We cannot undo the history that has already taken place. We can however seek to discover why at the parting of the ways on the eve of Nicea this Council chose the one way, did not take the alternative road and, having regard to the situation, could not do so. . . . In the long run the one-sided choice led to objections and misgivings which, the path once taken, have proved difficult to resolve" (B 570–71; italics added).

Chalcedon—"*In Jesus* God stands [add: personally—ed.] on our side of life; that after all is the gist of the Nicene dogma which affirms, does it not, the self-subsistent co-being of *the human being, Jesus*, with

---

2. But see the author's qualification on p. 565, end of first paragraph.

the Father.[3] The Council of Chalcedon, intending thereby to stress the true humanity of Jesus, says at the same time that this human being is set wholly on God's side. . . .[4] I have no trouble at all with any of this," the author continues, "seen from within a Greek intellectual outlook and the questions posed by it at that time; it is straight Gospel, but ... within a nexus of philosophical problems which is no longer in all respects entirely ours and indeed presents us nowadays with certain difficulties" (B 566–67 [italics in the Dutch original]).

When account is taken of the citations thus far given—1 and 2— in this section, is it inaccurate to say that for Fr. Schillebeeckx the dogmas of Nicea and Chalcedon have a *real* value because they are consistent with the norm and criterion, namely, Jesus as definitive messenger of God, Jesus in whom salvation comes to us from God, but also that their value is *relativized* in a way? Fr. Schillebeeckx himself tells us that "Christology is more relative (my italics [?]) than a 'theology of Jesus' " (B 549).[5] And he has told us (cf. above) that the teachings of Nicea and Chalcedon are truly valid by reason of their consistency with the Jesus of history—but it is a consistency within a horizon of understanding (an ideological context) proper to a particular age. In any case, more light will perhaps be thrown on the question.

3. *All interpretations subsequent to the experience and primordial response which history has uncovered.*—Let me allow Fr. Schillebeeckx to speak. A first statement seems to me to be ambiguous: "In that way a renewal of Christology will become possible within a new range of experi-

---

3. In point of fact, as far as "consubstantiality" is concerned the Council of Nicea does not lay the emphasis on "the human being, Jesus." It is Jesus as Son begotten before all ages who is "consubstantial" with the Father.

4. This is left rather vague. Fr. Schillebeeckx would have been better advised to say that the Council teaches that there is in Jesus a "person," "the only-begotten Son, the Word, our Lord Jesus Christ," and "two natures": the divine nature which he possesses before all the ages, and the human nature which he has from the time of his birth from the Virgin Mary, Mother of God (cf. *DS* 301, 302).

5. The hyphen within the word "theo-logy" is from the author's pen. I believe that for Fr. Schillebeeckx the term means here the idea of God which Jesus offers us: that of the God who in Jesus communicates salvation and makes his own the cause of human beings. ["My italics": it is likely that the writer of the Evaluation intended to italicize the words "more relative." In the original Schillebeeckx put "Christology" between inverted comma's, which the document omitted, quoting also the wrong page number.—Ed.]

ence and new categories of understanding, in which definitive and final salvation in Jesus, imparted by God [remark: but is that adequate?], is still encountered and still expressed" (B 571). Another statement seems to me likewise ambiguous: If one holds, says the author, that "in Jesus God saves man," one maintains "a primary and fundamental Christian orthodoxy" (Q 27; B 549). And similarly: "As a believer, one is bound by whatever Jesus entails, not directly by those articulating concepts" (Q 28; B 318). "Not directly": Does this mean: to the extent that in a given age and milieu they are necessary in order to maintain "a primary and fundamental Christian orthodoxy"? In any case, according to the Church the believer is directly bound, I would say, by the definitive Christological decisions of the magisterium.

Another passage seems to me to be, unfortunately, quite clear: "In its expression and in its content the dynamism of a faith which seeks to understand itself better leads it at one and the same time to a 'demythologization' that does away with existing formulations, and a 'remythologization' that develops new formulations. The permanent element in the content of faith is the *objectivity* of a mystery which transcends all expression but which nevertheless embodies itself in new formulations in keeping with the mobility of human existence" (Q 28; *Sept problèmes capitaux de l'Eglise* [Paris: Fayard, 1969], 106). Fr. Schillebeeckx offers no explanation with regard to this text, which is cited in the questionnaire, or to many of those reproduced in nos. 1, 2 and 3 of the present section.[6]

4. *An answer of Fr. Schillebeeckx* (R 71f).—Since Fr. Schillebeeckx admits a major change in Christological interpretations as a whole, we may ask how in his view the interpretation which he judges to be central and primordial can remain so stable. In this context the questionnaire refers to *two* distinctions proposed by the author: *one* (B 549)

---

6. In the last text cited there is a somewhat different nuance than in the preceding ones: the element which remains stable under differing expressions of the faith is not Jesus as definitive messenger from God or salvation coming from God but "the objectivity of a mystery which transcends all expression." Is the difference due to the earlier date of this last text (1969)? To some extent, perhaps. But (1) in this text there is question of faith in general and not, as in the other passages, of Christological faith; (2) there is, if not a wide bridge, at least a good foot-bridge between this text and the others. For the passage from a quite recent lecture that was cited earlier in the present section (B. The Christological interpretations..., no. 1, paragraph 5, p. 103) shows that behind the expressions "definitive messenger from God" and "salvation coming from God" lies an ineffable experience which to some extent finds a voice in them.

is between "first-order" assertions and "second-order" assertions (which are derived from the former); the *other* is between (a) "structural" ideas which are very stable and almost immutable, (b) "conjunctural" ideas which are less stable and change in the course of the ages, and, finally (c) "superficial" notions which are quite changeable (B 576–79). The questionnaire erroneously mixed the two distinctions together, and Fr. Schillebeeckx was justified in finding fault with it. I think that only the second distinction should have been brought into consideration. It enabled us to see that according to Fr. Schillebeeckx the Christology of Chalcedon belongs in a "conjunctural" horizon of understanding (B 578), whereas the central and primordial response of faith—a response he judges to be decidedly stable—might be classified by him among the "structural" ideas.

In any event, what has been said in nos. 1, 2 and 3 of the present section is independent of the mistake involved in the improper link between the *two* different distinctions which Fr. Schillebeeckx makes. In view of the texts cited in these three numbers—and less abundantly, but adequately, in the questionnaire (26f)—the fear of a certain dogmatic relativism continues to be founded.

According to Fr. Schillebeeckx, the questionnaire "reads into" his book "a [Christological] 'superposition' that is solely the work of the Church, *without objective basis* in Jesus himself" (R 74; italics mine) and that in no way reflects the meaning of his book. This erroneous reading seems to me non-existent. The questionnaire shows itself inclined, conditionally, to see the Nijmegen professor as saying that the central and primordial response of faith in Jesus was supplemented by other interpretative responses which indeed have *an objective foundation in Jesus,* but a foundation that makes them valid only within certain horizons of understanding. The fear voiced is admittedly a serious one, but it is based on texts of the author, and he has not yet explained these.

This experience (a faith experience) may very well be identical with "the dynamism of a faith which seeks to understand itself better" and which is in tension toward "the objectivity of a mystery which transcends all expression." The fact remains that the expressions "definitive messenger from God" and "salvation coming from God" are privileged as possessing a special stability. With regard to this point something more will be said as the evaluation continues. (The question of the interpretative responses made to revelation is treated at greater length by the author in his book: *The Understanding of Faith: Interpretation and Criticism,* tr. by N. D. Smith [New York, 1974; Dutch original, 1972].) (N. B. A considerably simpler explanation of the difference between the two texts is that the first one, of 1969, is not written by Schillebeeckx himself, but by the interviewer. Cf. Ch. I, Intro.—Ed.)

C. The messiahship of Jesus

With regard to a heading in the questionnaire: "Jesus (it is said) presented himself not as Messiah but as eschatological prophet" (Q 35), Fr. Schillebeeckx writes: "This opposition between 'not' and 'but' is nowhere to be found in my book" (R 79). He is mistaken, for in a passage to which the questionnaire refers, he writes: "In his life on earth [which alone is at issue, since the questionnaire does not doubt at all that Fr. Schillebeeckx—like everyone else—admits that in the post-Easter community Jesus was acknowledged as royal heavenly Messiah] Jesus acts, *not* in a messianic role *but* as the eschatological prophet" (B 245; italics mine). [When one compares this quote with its French translation, one can see that it has been sharpened—ed.] Admittedly—and the questionnaire takes this into account—the author adds: "and that, according to one particular Jewish tradition, is equally 'messianic' " (*ibid.*).

What is the point here? According to the common Jewish view at the time of Jesus the Messiah was to be the mighty liberator king of the last times and also a prophet (cf., e.g., Jn 6:14). This king was described in nationalistic and political terms; since he was to be king and prophet, the emphasis could be placed on either the first or the second of these two titles. People also envisaged messianic prophets who would act as precursor or assistant to the Messiah; but I shall not dwell on this, because Fr. Schillebeeckx is not thinking of such figures. In one tradition, which is attested weakly and in rather vague form, there was the idea of a messianic prophet, who would be, if we might so put it, a *substitute* for the royal Messiah (cf. perhaps Jn 1:20–21), the *kingship* of the Messiah being *eliminated*. Finally, according to the greatest number of exegetes Jesus effected a new messianic synthesis; he gave it to be understood (especially to his disciples at the end of his life) that he intended to be *the royal Messiah*, the *Son of man who would reign in glory*, but after having suffered, and then in a fashion that was not political but religious and full of mystery.

The questionnaire adopts the last-named position and says that it is not the position of Fr. Schillebeeckx, who holds rather the preceding view: an eschatological prophet (who claims no kingship, even of a transcendent kind), a prophet therefore who may still be called messianic—but only one who is a *substitute* for the royal Messiah.

The questionnaire has a number of reasons for attributing this position to Fr. Schillebeeckx. (1) Unless I am mistaken, nowhere in his book does the author say that Jesus, who presented himself as the eschatological prophet, also presented himself in some fashion or other as a royal Messiah. (I note that in his response he alleges no text that would support this second claim.) (2) Fr. Schillebeeckx challenges the historicity or relevance of all the Gospel passages that might justify the thesis that Jesus intended to fulfill in his own way the expectation of a royal Messiah: the confession of Peter (B 320–423); the fact that Jesus spoke of himself as the Son of man according to Daniel (Dan 7:13–14); the entry of Jesus into Jerusalem with its messianic trappings (see Zech 9:9) (it seems to me, in fact, that Fr. Schillebeeckx has passed over in silence the entry into Jerusalem); the cleansing of the temple (B 243–45); the condemnation of Jesus by the Sanhedrin because of his claim to a transcendent messiahship (B 315); the condemnation of Jesus by Pilate as "king of the Jews" (B 316–17), and this although the notice attached to the cross bears all the signs of authenticity (but the author makes no mention of it). (3) In agreement with Bultmann and a few other writers, Fr. Schillebeeckx says several times (B 148, 469) that Jesus announced the Son of man in Daniel as a figure *distinct from himself* and whose coming he himself awaited. But, of course, it is this Son of man who receives from God the power to reign forever (Dan 7:14). If then we conceive him as being an individual person and not a symbol for the Jewish people (cf. Dan 7:18)—and in the common opinion of exegetes, including Fr. Schillebeeckx, that is how Jesus conceived him—the Son of man can only be a *transcendent royal Messiah* (which does not prevent him from being Davidic as well).[7] But if Jesus awaited this personage, this messianic and kingly Son of man, *as someone distinct from himself,* he could not have conceived of himself as a prophet and Messiah king.

In his response Fr. Schillebeeckx claims to have expressly indicated in his book that Jesus had "the role of eschatological messianic prophet," and in support of his claim he refers to page 477 of his book. Now he does say this in the passage to which he refers, but he is speaking there of what Jesus was in the eyes of the post-Easter community which identified him (we are told) with the Son of man—contrary (need I repeat it?) to what, according to Fr. Schillebeeckx, Jesus really meant. At the same time, Fr. Schillebeeckx says his entire book shows that after the death of the Lord the disciples believed and made explicit "what Jesus himself in fact was and said" (R 80). This is odd

---

7. In the two books from the time of Jesus that speak of Daniel's Son of man (or simply Man), namely, the parables in the Book of Enoch and the Apocalypse of Esdras, the Son of man is conceived as being a transcendent royal Messiah.

indeed: for it would have been by contradicting him that the disciples explicitated what Jesus said of his relation to the Son of man in Daniel.

Though I do not wish to be overly dramatic, I think it is not a minor matter to deny that Jesus had a royal messianic purpose of a mysterious kind (this is not simply to be hypercritical). For kingship was *a persistent element in the messianic prophecies.* The harmony of the two Testaments, which faith requires us to safeguard, seems to me to be in question here. Nor is it a minor matter to say that Jesus awaited the Son of man as a personage distinct from himself and that the post-Easter community identified him with this personage. What a strange beginning for the development of Christology, a development which we are told is legitimate!

D. Jesus, "Servant of Yahweh"

The questionnaire says: "It is your view, Reverend Father, that in none of the predictions of his passion did Jesus refer to his death as sacrificial and propitiatory (B 311). In order to be able to maintain this position, you must refuse to attribute to Jesus certain *logia* which enjoy a better fate in the hands of many exegetes" (Q 37). To this opening observation Fr. Schillebeeckx makes no answer. Very well. The questionnaire continues: "More serious still, you are led to deny even that the words of eucharistic institution, as far as those elements in them are concerned which are common to Paul and the Synoptics, can be regarded as historical (B 308)" (Q 37).

Fr. Schillebeeckx answers by referring to this very passage of the questionnaire (Q 37), but in doing so he makes its language vaguer. He asks where in his book one may see a denial "that 'the words of eucharistic institution' (Dossier, 37) have their basis in the history of Jesus."

Let us answer by repeating the words of the questionnaire: "You are led to deny even that the words of eucharistic institution, as far as those elements in them are concerned which are common to Paul and the Synoptics, can be regarded as historical (B 308)." On page 308 Fr. Schillebeeckx speaks in terms which do not seem to me susceptible of more than one meaning. He is dealing here with the very texts of eucharistic institution to which the questionnaire refers, and he says (the italics are mine): "That these passages have been influenced by liturgical practice in the Church *and so* have a post-Easter stamp upon them is *clear* enough. But in both Luke (22:18) and Mark (14:25) one can detect an older vein, which according to F. Hahn belongs 'to the primeval rock (*Urgestein*) of the tradition,' as scholars nowadays almost universally agree: 'Truly I say to you, I shall not drink again of the fruit of the vine until that day when I drink it new in the Kingdom of God' " (B 308).—In short, the *post-Easter* character of the words of institution is *clear*, but a verse about the wine which Jesus will not drink again except in the Kingdom of God is also found in the narrative of the Supper, and the latter is historical. It is historical, I say, but again a distinction must be made. Whatever value Fr. Schillebeeckx may assign to the text in question, his view is that the second half of it (the first half is the statement that Jesus will not drink again of the fruit of the vine; the second is that he will however drink it "new" in the Kingdom of God)—his view, I say, is that this second half "has another source" and that the "combination" of the two utterances "is clearly secondary" (B 309).[8]

All of this is decidedly negative, but Fr. Schillebeeckx is not disturbed by it, because the attitude of Jesus in offering a final cup to his disciples while announcing his imminent death must be seen in the light of the earlier life of the Master; when thus viewed it means that "even prior to Easter Jesus is saying, in effect at any rate, that the 'Jesus affair' is to go ahead" (B 311); and this, he says, "is a very important conclusion."

"A very important conclusion"? Perhaps so. The fact remains, however, that the questionnaire seems to have been quite justified in saying to Fr. Schillebeeckx: "You are led to deny even that the words of eucharistic institution, as far as those elements in them are concerned which are common to Paul and the Synoptics, can be regarded as historical" (Q 37; cf. above).[9]

---

8. In 1969 Fr. Schillebeeckx had already spoken very briefly in the same negative vein about the words of eucharistic institution: "Historically speaking, moreover, the whole theology of the Eucharist originated from the disciples' reflection on their eating together with Christ. The Eucharist did not originate as it were abstractly from a word of Christ or some such thing. [But there is nothing abstract about the words of Christ over the bread and wine as these are reported as having been spoken on the eve of his death during a meal which was at least a substitute for the passover meal.] It originated rather in the practice of eating with one another and with Christ, and later in remembrance of Christ. [If I believed this, I do not see how I could still remain attached to the celebration of the Eucharist]" (*The Crucial Questions on Problems Facing the Church Today*, 84). I judge that what I might well call the author's hypercritical attitude on the subject of eucharistic institution is very dangerous to the faith.

9. In his response Fr. Schillebeeckx also says that with Professor Schürmann he makes a "distinction between two textual strata in the New Testament" as far as the account of the Supper is concerned, the two being most clear in Luke. True enough,

But let me get back to the Servant of Yahweh. Fr. Schillebeeckx thinks that "neither the veiled ... nor the open predictions of the Passion [by Jesus] ... contain any allusion to the death as salvation or propitiation" (B 310–11; cf. also above, at the beginning of this section). For good measure, one might say, he thinks that "Jesus at the Last Supper passes the cup—the last one—to his friends and so *continues* [italics in the Dutch original] to offer a saving fellowship with himself, 'in spite of' his approaching death" (B 310)—in spite of this death, but also till in his death (B 311). Finally—I am still conveying Fr. Schillebeeckx' views—it is legitimate to say of Jesus "that—*not comprehending it, perhaps* [italics mine], but as a heartfelt conviction— he integrated this death into his proffer of salvation, the point and purpose of his whole life" (B 542). In view of all this, I think it impossible to maintain that in the author's view Jesus *intended* to be the "Servant of Yahweh" in the sense this term has in the fourth Servant song of Second Isaiah (52:13—53:12)—a song according to which this personage seeks to expiate by his death for the sins of mankind: "My servant will justify the multitudes by taking the burden of their sin upon himself. ... He gave himself up to death ... and ... he interceded for the guilty" (Is 53:11–12). In the perspective adopted by Fr. Schillebeeckx one may certainly call Jesus the Servant of Yahweh by reason of the *service* he rendered as messenger from God (although the title "Servant of God" occurs very infrequently in his book); but it is not possible to say that within himself—in his "offer"—Jesus intended to accept death as a form of satisfaction or as a sacrifice of propitiation for sins. Yet the author claims that in his book he offers a

---

but the questionnaire did not query him on this matter, which is open to discussion (L. Cerfaux and P. Benoit disagree with Schürmann). Fr. Schillebeeckx finds fault with the questionnaire for saying that he follows Marxsen in his historico-critical interpretation of the Supper, whereas in fact he does not even mention Marxsen. We answer: (1) this is irrelevant to the substance of the question raised above; (2) the statement of the questionnaire is meant to refer primarily to W. Marxsen's little book, *Das Abendmahl als christologisches Problem* (Gütersloh, 1963; ET: *The Lord's Supper as a Christological Problem*, published together with Marxsen's *The Beginnings of Christology* [Philadelphia, 1979]), which created not a little stir; (3) Fr. Schillebeeckx' conclusions are very close to those of Marxsen; (4) he does not mention Marxsen here, but he will perhaps recall that in 1966 he wrote that, while not letting himself be drawn so far as to agree completely with Marxsen's interpretation of the eucharistic texts (in the short book just cited), he did however wish "to draw attention with some emphasis to certain points contained in his [traditio-historical] analysis," an analysis supplemented by a study of B. van Iersel (Schillebeeckx, *Christus' tegenwoordigheid in de Eucharistie* [Bilthoven: Nelissen, 1966], 96–97; ET: *The Eucharist*, tr. by N. D. Smith, [New York, 1968], 122).—I believe, nonetheless, that the questionnaire would have done better to drop the reference to Marxsen, since it was pointless.

"critique of dogma" which is "that of a believing Christian who, starting from the 'earthly Jesus,' wants to test and check (*toetsen*) the notions ['notions' italicized in the Dutch original.—Ed.] current in the Church and among Christians about the relevance to salvation of Jesus' death, in order to see whether in a Christian soteriology we are *tied* [italics in the original] to concepts like 'ransom' [Mk 10:45; 1 Pet 1:18], 'propitiation' [1 Jn 2:2; 4:10; Eph 5:2], 'substitution' [2 Cor 5:21; Gal 3:13; 1 Pet 2:24], 'satisfaction' (= reparation) [Rom 5:18–19] and so forth" (B 318).

What response does Fr. Schillebeeckx make? *First:* "I expressly say that these eucharistic texts *faithfully represent* the *historical* actions and *words* of Christ" (Dutch, 253; English, 308)" (R 81). The only statement on this page (253) of the book that resembles even a little what is claimed here is the following: "The passage [i.e., the verse which Fr. Schillebeeckx has just cited and which he regards as historical: 'From now on I shall not drink of the fruit of the vine until the Kingdom of God comes': Lk 22:15–18; cf. 1 Cor 11:26] contains two elements: (1) on the one hand, a main feature of this meal is the— at any rate—quite emphatic announcement by Jesus of his imminent death; in other words: this meal is a farewell to all such earthly fellowship (it really is the very last cup that Jesus will share with his friends); (2) on the other hand, Jesus offers it with the prospect of fellowship renewed in the Kingdom of God.[10] The 'words of institution' mentioned above, in the context of the Church's liturgy, would appear to state these rather more vague pronouncements in a more precise and explicit form" (B 308). I do not see how the eucharistic texts, the words pronounced over the bread and wine as reported by Paul and the Synoptics, "faithfully represent the historical actions and words of Christ" (R 81). Father Schillebeeckx says that "neither the veiled ... nor the open predictions of the Passion [by Jesus] ... contain any allusion to the death as salvation or propitiation" (B 310–11). But the eucharistic texts in question do contain the idea of sacrifice.

Second: For further explanation Fr. Schillebeeckx refers to his quite recent book: *Christ: The Experience of Jesus as Lord* (New York, 1980; Dutch original, 1977). After a careful investigation I can say that the author does expound there the propitiatory and sacrificial soteriologies of the New Testament writers (and a good deal else besides).

---

10. On the next page of his book (309) Fr. Schillebeeckx has to explain—as we saw earlier—that in the verse cited the part referring to the eschatological banquet comes not from the historical Last Supper but from another source.

But I have not seen him saying—and this is precisely the question—
that these soteriologies have their justification in the "offer" of Jesus;
that they are more than "interpretative responses" which are appropriate to changed horizons of understanding; that they still demand
our assent of faith. In fact, I have found there rather the contrary. It
would, of course, be utterly unjust to judge a book of 925 pages—
what astounding energy and capacity for work!—by a single passage.
But since the author refers us to this work without indicating a specific passage (that kind of indication was probably still impossible at
the time he wrote his response), I shall cite a rather general statement
which I do not find really surprising in the context of the entire exposition: "So for believers, *revelation* is an *action of God* as *experienced* by
believers and *interpreted* in religious language, and therefore expressed in human terms, in the dimension of our utterly human history. The all-pervasive, authoritative element of revelation in this
complex context is not this interpretative experience itself but what
can be experienced in it [=in the interpretative experience]" (78; the
italics are the author's).

One final remark. The questionnaire cites a passage in which Fr.
Schillebeeckx says: "First, I would dare to say that we are saved *despite* the death of Jesus, in spite of it! Second, I would only add that
such language is in the final analysis somewhat inadequate" (Q 39).
He explains this by saying that Jesus accepted his death by filling it
with his love for the Father and for human beings and that for this
reason God raised him up, so that "we are really brought to salvation
in and through the love-unto-death which Jesus had" (H. Kuitert and
E. Schillebeeckx, *Jezus van Nazareth en het heil van de wereld* [Baarn:
Ten Have, 1975], 38–39). This is something, I would say, but it is far
from being enough. For, *first of all*, we may not forget that according
to the author Jesus, "not comprehending it *perhaps* . . . integrated [his]
death into his proffer of salvation, the point and purpose of his whole
life" (B 542, and above in this section). *Furthermore*, the New Testament does not say that Jesus saved us basically *despite* his death:
"Christ died for our sins in accordance with the Scriptures" (1 Cor
15:3); "[Jesus] was put to death for our trespasses and raised for our
justification" (Rom 4:25); "[Jesus said:] 'Lo, I have come to do thy
will.' . . . And by that will we have been sanctified through the offering of the body of Jesus Christ once for all" (Heb 10:9–10); and so on.
Not only that, but the author refuses to say that God willed to hand
Jesus over to death. "God," he says, "is not checkmated by what
men—not God himself—did to Jesus, namely, put him to death" (in
the passage just cited in part from the book of H. Kuitert and E.

Schillebeeckx); and again: "This really places the suffering [of Jesus] *outside* of God and leaves it inside the mundane sphere of legitimacy.... In and over against Jesus God evidently remains sovereignly free ... something that applies to every child of man" (B 651). This, I would note, is not in agreement with St. Paul: "[God] did not spare his own Son but gave him up for us all" (Rom 8:32), nor with St. John: "[God] sent his Son to be the expiation for our sins" (1 Jn 4:10), nor with the fourth song of the Servant of Yahweh: "Yahweh willed to crush him with suffering: if he offers his life as a sacrifice of expiation, he will see a posterity, he will prolong his days" (Is 53:10).

I think we may conclude that Jesus himself, Jesus in his "offer," is not, as presented by Fr. Schillebeeckx, "the suffering Servant of Yahweh."

E. Jesus and his Father

The questionnaire recognizes that for Fr. Schillebeeckx the experience which Jesus had of God as Abba (beloved Father) was "the soul, source and ground of Jesus' message, praxis and ministry as a whole"; that it "evidently goes deeper than the purely prophetic consciousness"; and that it begins "to prompt theological questions" (Q 41f; B 259). It admits that in this area, according to the author, the Jesus of history provides a basis for the Christology developed in the New Testament (Q 42f). But it adds that the basis is a "weak" one (*ibid.*) because of an excessively negative criticism of many passages in the Synoptics. Fr. Schillebeeckx says that he is truly pained by this judgment (R 81), although he perhaps does not fully realize how much of the positive there is in the judgment. The Congregation for the Doctrine of the Faith regrets having caused him this pain, but it cannot avoid noting certain points.

1. On at least several occasions Jesus invokes God under the name "Abba." The invocation makes use of a word which in secular usage was reserved almost completely, as regards its use in dialogue, for the family circle: a person would address his own father in this manner. Some very detailed studies (cf. especially J. Jeremias and W. Marchel) have shown—and no one has thus far demonstrated the contrary—that in Jewish usage people *never* addressed God in this manner (Christians did so [Gal 4:4–6; Rom 8:15], but with an awareness that they were able to exercise such a holy daring only because of the Spirit of Jesus who inspired them [*ibid.*]). Why then does Fr. Schillebeeckx, without citing any text, say that in the Jewish world God was

addressed as Abba in "a few cases (which point of course to a new ten-dency)" (B 260)? It is not surprising, given this statement, to find him saying: "Thus that Jesus should say *Abba* to God—apart from the great solemnity, holding God at a distance as it were [but the entire psalter contradicts this!], with which people in Jesus' time used to pray to him—makes no essential difference" (B 259). To these quite specific observations of the questionnaire (Q 40–42) Fr. Schillebeeckx has made no response.

2. The questionnaire says that in regard to the passages in which Jesus attributes divine prerogatives to himself (passages which deserve to be taken into consideration) or others such as the so-called "hymn of jubiliation" and the parable of the murderous vineyard workers (the "servants" and the "son"), the author is excessively negative in his criticism. There are points that are open to debate, but I think that the observation in the questionnaire is justified.

3. Finally, according to the author Jesus "never posited himself (beside the rule of God) as the second object of his preaching" (B 258). The author acknowledges that "disagreement is possible on [this] statement," but he adds that he thinks it is "justified" "at the historical level" (R 82). But it can be regarded as "justified" only if one denies that Jesus gradually made known a messianic synthesis in which he is the royal Messiah, though in a new sense of the term, and in which he is also at once the Son of man of Daniel and the Servant of Yahweh of the Book of Isaiah. The denial is one which I regard as lacking in any solid critical basis.

All in all, it does not seem to me that the questionnaire was overly rigid. In any event, while judging that the author had weakened (I would by no means say: done away with) the "apologetic" foundation of Christology, the questionnaire does not find him guilty of any doctrinal error in his historical study of the relations between Jesus and his Father.

F. On "hypostatic identification"

This section on the "hypostatic identification" of which the author speaks will be divided into *two parts*. The *first*—which is concerned directly with the word "hypostatic" ("hypostasis" and "person" are used as synonyms in the Council of Chalcedon)—will deal with the fact that Fr. Schillebeeckx speaks of "Jesus, a human person." The *second*, connected directly with the word "identification," will deal with the way in which the author understands the relation he establishes between what he calls the "human person of Jesus" and the Word of God.

1. *Jesus, a human person.*—Almost at the beginning of his great work, Fr. Schillebeeckx writes that "the man Jesus, in the human sense of the word, is a human person" [literal translation of the French; in the Dutch original it is a parenthesis, without the "is," and "human person" is between inverted commas, p. 26, like the English version: "That the man Jesus, in the sense of 'a human person,' is for me the starting point . . ." p. 33.—Tr.]. He adds that it is a "truism" (B 33) because "there are no ghosts or gods in disguise wandering around in our human history; only people" (*ibid.*). Was the questionnaire not justified, therefore, in thinking that this was his own view?

Since, moreover, he offered this statement as "the starting point of all my reflections (*bezinning*)" (*ibid.*), and since it precedes the four main parts that comprise the book *Jesus: An Experiment in Christology*, the questionnaire could say to him, quite circumspectly, it seems to me: "This 'starting point,' which is made explicit in your introduction, *seems* [italics mine] to inspire both your exegesis and your dogmatic theology" (Q 30).

But in the last analysis what does Fr. Schillebeeckx mean by his statement, which is only imperfectly explained by obviously caricatural expressions that dismiss "ghosts" and "gods in disguise" from the world around us? Since "Jesus, a human person," is a "starting point" of "all my reflection" (*ibid.*) in this book, the questionnaire was justified in presuming that the expression would have the same meaning throughout the book—the primary issue is the meaning of the word "person"—at least when the author is expressing his own thought. I say "presuming," while bearing in mind, of course, the adage *praesumptio cedit veritati* (presumption yields to fact).

In any case, the questionnaire begins by offering the author the following interpretation, which is meant as a kind of suggestion. The statement that Jesus is a human person might be interpreted as meaning by "person" that "Jesus possesses a genuine, intelligent and free human subjectivity, while not denying [or affirming] that this subjectivity . . . is in continuity with an ultimate subjectivity, that of the eternal Word" (Q 30). The questionnaire then mentions an expression which Fr. Schillebeeckx applies to Jesus as a man (in the fourth part of his book): "a humanly conscious center of action and human . . . freedom" (B 667). And the questionnaire observes that if this expres-

sion is regarded as a key and if "center" is understood not as an ultimate "center" but as a center and subjectivity that is "perhaps simply
proximate," then the statement that was taken as a "starting point"
for the investigation undertaken in the book as a whole would be defensible, despite its being unusual when compared with traditional
theological language (Q 30).

The questionnaire had all the more reason for "suggesting" this
interpretation because in the passage already cited Fr. Schillebeeckx
speaks of what the man Jesus is "in the human sense" (meaning "usual sense"?) of the word "man." Yet it was difficult to offer more than
a suggestion along this line. For Fr. Schillebeeckx had taken care to
supply a lexicon defining a series of terms which he uses. And in this
lexicon he defines a person as "a complete (*afgerond*), independent
(*zelfstandig*), self-subsistent (*op zich staande*) existence" (B 743). With
this definition he places himself in the theological tradition, especially that of St. Thomas (it would admittedly have been good for him to
add that this existing being is "intellectual" and free, but that is surely what he has in mind). And he himself notes on page 664 of his book
that St. Thomas' idea of person is in agreement with that of "the 'linguistic analysis' of *today*" (italics mine).

Even if we understand "person" in this way, we can, in keeping,
if not with the habitual language of theologians, at least with the traditional doctrine itself, say that Jesus is a human person. This can be
said, and once again the questionnaire says it—as a kind of suggestion—provided we are looking at the person not from the standpoint
of the elements *which constitute it* as an ultimate subject but from the
standpoint of that which, as an ultimate subject, it *possesses* (cf. Q 31).
The divine person of the Son of God possesses a humanity in virtue
of the Incarnation, and for that reason it is a human person, just as it
is a person who preached and suffered and was raised up (*ibid.*).

But Fr. Schillebeeckx refuses to yield to the suggestions of the
questionnaire. Instead he blames it for having given an "ontological"
meaning to the word "person" in his "starting point": "Jesus, a human person" (R 63). But he forgets to take into account that the meaning given to the word person in the questionnaire is the meaning—
the only meaning—given to it in his own lexicon; and that the questionnaire says that it is making use of the lexicon (Q 30).[11]—On this

---

11. I confess that I do not see how a definition of the person—the person being at
least an intelligent and free being (or an "end in itself")—can fail to be "ontological," at
least implicitly and even though the definer may deny it.

point he has not responded. In addition, he shows himself allergic to the traditional idea that Jesus is not, in his humanity, a person in the sense of a subject which is closed in upon itself in the line of subjectivity. For when he speaks of an "anhypostasis" that would be proper to the humanity of Jesus ("anhypostasis" = lacking [alpha privative] in a subsistence of its own), inasmuch as the hypostasis of this humanity is to be found only in a divine subject, namely the Word of God (B 746)—when, I say, he speaks of such an anhypostasis, he shows himself immediately opposed to it; and the only reason he offers for this opposition is that "this at any rate suggests that Christ is not a human being 'complete and unabridged' " (*ibid.*; cf. B 569, par. 2).[12]

A final remark of Fr. Schillebeeckx. He stresses the point that he is speaking "only of two phases or stages in the journey of the disciples: (1) the first meeting and their first impression, and (2) the final impression after the death of Jesus (this final impression takes the form of an act of faith in which Jesus is ultimately identified in an ontological way: as the Son of God). "The purpose of my book," he says, "was in fact grasped by all my readers" (R 63). I do not doubt it; but I do not understand why he believes that what all his readers grasped, the questionnaire failed to grasp. The questionnaire *never* asks that in his historical inquiry he take as the starting point of his argument the fact that Jesus is the Son of God made man or the fact that once they had been greatly enlightened by their experience of Easter and their further reflection under the influence of the Spirit, the apostles understood and expressed the incarnation differently than they had during the course of a confusing and difficult journey. *Nor* does it ask him to base his argument, in this historical investigation, on the fact that the person of Jesus is the person of the Word of God rather than a human person. The only point it criticizes is that the mystery of the person of Christ seems to be challenged by an opening statement (B 33) when this is read in the light of the author's own lexicon.

But, as the author says in his response (R 76), in the "provisional synthesis" which is given in the fourth part of his book, he does explain "at the ontological level" his thinking about the person of Jesus. Let us follow him in this final step. My argument will be rather fine-

---

12. After all, if we overlook the caricatural nature of the expression, there is some resemblance between a God "disguised" as a man (B 33; cf. beginning of this section) and the Word of God who supposedly assumed a human nature, yet "was not a human being 'complete and unabridged.' "

spun at one or other point. I would ask pardon for this, if the responsibility for it were mine, but in fact it is the author who is responsible.

2. *"Some such thing as a 'hypostatic identification' without anhypostasis"* (B 667). This title consists of some words from Fr. Schillebeeckx. What do the words mean?

At issue is the "identification" of the Word and the human nature of Jesus, but an "identification" in which it is understood that this nature is not in "a condition from which 'being-a-human-person' (*menselijk persoon-zijn*) is absent" (B 746). And in order to make sure that he is properly understood, the author adds that the "anhypostasis" which he *excludes* (cf. above, and also below *passim*) would imply "that Jesus does indeed have a human nature and (in that sense) is a human being, but that his being-*qua*-person is constituted by the divine person [of the Word]" (B 746). He adds, further, that the anhypostasis—which, let me repeat, he rejects—implies that "Christ is not a human person" (*ibid.*).

Let me say something first about "(hypostatic) *identification*"; then I shall speak of this "identification" insofar as it is said to be *"without anhypostasis."*

The questionnaire asks whether hypostatic "identification" is to be understood as meaning an identity pure and simple or rather an ineffable union. The questionnaire indicates briefly (Q 46) that if the first alternative is chosen, one immediately falls into monophysism. In his response Fr. Schillebeeckx does not object to this conclusion at all; this already suggests that he understands "hypostatic identification" as meaning an "ineffable union." More than this, he says that to speak of hypostatic identification is to speak "falteringly," and he adds, in parentheses: "I prefer this term to *unio hypostatica*" (B 667).[13] The ineffable union alternative is thus not excluded, and do we not in the end come back to the traditional "hypostatic union" (even if expressed in a different formula)? That is what Fr. Schillebeeckx claims in his response (he did not say it in his book): "In my judgment, this [the expression 'hypostatic identification'] restates the traditional hy-

---

13. Why? He does not say. But in a 1966 article (*Tijdschrift voor Theologie* 6 [1966] 283, n. 14), in which he already speaks of "hypostatic identity" and defends a position that will later be spelled out in his book, he writes: "[The expression "hypostatic union"] is too suggestive of pre-existing components." This remark is very debatable, and it might be said in reply that "hypostatic *identity*" suggests a kind of monophysism.—But, let me repeat, I do not believe that the author holds a form of monophysism.

postatic union in its purest form" (R 78). In the final analysis, it seems to me prudent to opt for the alternative to which the questionnaire was inclined, namely, that "hypostatic identification" means not an absolute identity but an ineffable union.

Is it also the case that it coincides with "the traditional hypostatic union"? My question is concerned, of course, not with the intention or subjective thought of the author but with the objective meaning of the book. Well, I am unfortunately certain—for the texts seem to me to be compelling—that this objective meaning does not convey the doctrine according to which Jesus—whose human nature is not a person (it does not subsist in itself)—exists in the Word as its ultimate subject: a divine subsistent being, distinct from the Father and the Spirit, the second Person of the Most Holy Trinity. I am aware of how serious my statement is, since the doctrine to which I am referring is part of the Catholic faith. I am also aware that after the contrary statement of the author (one unfortunately not accompanied by texts that would justify it) I have an obligation to furnish proofs. The questionnaire has already provided two, to which I shall come back, but I shall provide others as well. I shall provide them by reference to the title I have given to this second part of the present section: "some such thing as a 'hypostatic identification' without anhypostasis," which is taken verbatim from Fr. Schillebeeckx' book (B 667). I shall provide them, in other words, as I ask in what this hypostatic identification (which is an "ineffable union") without anhypostasis" consists.

a. What does the author[14] mean by saying that the "identification" of the Word with the human nature of Jesus is "without anhypostasis"? His answer is clear. "Anhypostasis," he explains, means (since the prefix an- contains an alpha privative) "a condition from which 'being-a-human-person' (*menselijk persoon zijn*) is absent."[15] "It is implied," he continues, "that Jesus does indeed have a human nature and (in that sense) is a human being, but that his being-*qua*-person (*persoon-zijn*) is constituted by the divine person." Yes, and, I would point out, it is the meaning of the Council of Chalcedon (*DS*

---

14. In fact, the author and not a few recent theologians.

15. Fr. Schillebeeckx observes, quite rightly, that the word "absence" is "neutral." Several times he speaks less properly (or improperly) of a "deprivation of human *personal* being" ([literally: "loss of (a) human person"] *menselijk persoonsverlies*) (B 764) or of a "lack" ("something was lacking": B 569). I say he speaks less properly (or improperly), because these expressions are pejorative and by using them he gives himself an unearned advantage. The advantage is unearned because the absence in Christ of a human person (subsistence), when joined to the existence of his humanity in and through the divine subsistence of the Word, is unqualifiedly a supereminent perfection.

301–2), the second Council of Constantinople (*DS* 425, 426, 428), and the fourth Lateran Council (*DS* 801). But, by refusing to accept "anhypostasis," Fr. Schillebeeckx directly opposes this meaning.[16]

b. The questionnaire calls attention to the fact that Fr. Schillebeeckx speaks of an "enhypostasis" (personalization in another person) that was "mutual" (*wederkerige enhypostasie*) between the humanity of Jesus and the Word and that deepened up to the resurrection (Q 47; B 667). Whether this be the intention or not, this statement implies the existence in Jesus of two persons: the humanity and the Word, with each receiving the other and each thus achieving personalization in the other. At this point Fr. Schillebeeckx makes a slight—very slight—concession: "I simply acknowledge," he says, "after rereading the entire context, that my formula 'mutual enhypostasis' may in fact be ambiguous, especially to Scholastic minds" (R 87). He then adds that he is dealing with what the Greek Fathers call "perichoresis" and "theandrism" (*ibid.*). But as far as I know, the Greek Fathers are speaking (quite legitimately) of an intra-Trinitarian "perichoresis." As far as I know (but my knowledge in this area is very limited), only Nestorians made use of a "perichoresis" between the Word and the humanity of Jesus in order to explain the (inadequate) union which they established between the two *prosôpa* of Christ. As for "theandrism," the term is used by a good number of Greek Fathers, but it applies to the level of *activities* and not that of the "identity" or the hypostatic union in the Word made man (cf. the Lateran Council of 649, under Pope Martin I, at which a *theandrikē* activity, understood as a unique activity [without the participation of two wills] in Christ, was condemned; *DS* 515).—In my opinion Fr. Schillebeeckx' answer is inadequate.

c. It is true that in his Response (87) he adds a further explana-

---

16. Fr. Schillebeeckx does not deny that according to the teaching of the Council of Constantinople II the humanity of Jesus is not a hypostasis. It would be foolhardy to deny it, since in two of its canons (*DS* 425, 426) the Council says so in so many words. But why does he nowhere (as far as I know) speak of this Council? As far as the Council of Chalcedon is concerned, he thinks (B 569) that it does not exclude the idea of a person or hypostasis proper to the humanity of Jesus. But, in all honesty, this seems an unacceptable interpretation. For the Council explicitly says in its definition that in Jesus there is only one person or hypostasis who has two natures: the divinity and the humanity, and the person in question is called "the only-begotten Son, the Word who is God, our Lord Jesus Christ" (*DS* 301, 302). Is that not clear enough? It is the person of the Word who possesses the divinity from all eternity and who has assumed the humanity within time. In his book *Jesus the Christ* (New York, 1976), 237ff, W. Kasper unhesitatingly recognizes that in this case Constantinople II further specified Chalcedon in a legitimate way.

tion: "The person of the Logos envelops the entire personalist (= formally spiritual) humanity of Jesus and ... this concrete humanity does not remain extrinsic to or outside of the hypostasis of the Logos" (R *ibid.*). But it is clear, in my opinion, that while this explanation does justice to the "enhypostasis" of the humanity of Jesus in the Word, it does not explain at all the *"mutual* enhypostasis" which would include the personalization of the Word by the humanity of Jesus. And the proof that in the book this "mutual enhypostasis" cannot be taken in the harmless sense it is given in Fr. Schillebeeckx' Response, is that just after affirming this mutual enhypostasis in his book, the author continues: "In this respect (*hierbij*) Jesus stands *over against* the Father and the Spirit; not however *over against* the Son of God. ... [Yet in the end] we cannot (without all sorts of qualifications) describe him as simply and solely [the French phrase 'tout court' is used in the Dutch original] a 'human person,' for then there would indeed appear an inconceivable *'over against'* between the man Jesus and the Son of God" (B 667; italics in the Dutch original).

Remarks: In all truth, if the humanity of Jesus is personalized by its union with the Word and in turn personalizes the Word (!), there is no longer an unchanged "over against" (I and Thou) between it and the Word. The words of the author which I cited a moment ago show how seriously he takes his disconcerting "mutual enhypostasis." I conclude, then, that according to his book there are in Jesus two hypostases (the human and the divine) which reciprocally personalize one another. I conclude also that "the human person of Jesus"—his humanity "without anhypostasis" (B 667, and the citation which forms the title for this entire section)—continues to be affirmed—but not "without all sorts of qualifications." Unfortunately, I am compelled to add that a theology truly faithful to the Council of Chalcedon and to its unvarying interpretation in the Church should not state—even "with all sorts of qualifications"—that the humanity of Jesus has its own hypostasis.

d. The author refuses to admit that Jesus Christ as a subject can have two components: the humanity and the divinity: "What is more, however intimately this union with God is displayed in an historical human being, we can never speak of two components: humanity *and* divinity" (B 655; the context shows he is speaking of Jesus).—Yet this is precisely what one must acknowledge, if one admits that in Jesus the person of the Word has two natures, "unconfused and unseparated," to use the terms of Chalcedon (*DS* 302). St. Thomas asserts the same when he gives an affirmative answer to the question: "Is the person of Christ a composite one?" (*Summa theol.* III, q. 2, a. 4). The

Angelic Doctor is not saying anything new here, for, to say nothing of older patristic and theological testimonies, the Second Council of Chalcedon had already taught in its fourth canon that "the unity of the Word of God with the flesh which was animated by a rational and intellectual soul was accomplished by composition (*kata synthesin*)" and that we must confess "one composite hypostasis, which is the Lord Jesus Christ" (*DS* 424; cf. 425 and 428).—Once again, this composition in a single person is the logical consequence of the Word of God being united to a human nature that has no hypostasis of its own and is not a human person.

e. The questionnaire cites a statement which Fr. Schillebeeckx made in a conversation with J. Spitz (who is entirely on his side and has published the conversation *Kosmos & Oekumene* 8 [1974] 185): "The Christology of about a decade ago, which is still set forth in preaching, is no longer persuasive. People now resist the Christ-as-object-of-worship presented to them in such an exaggeratedly divinized form. I too am puzzled by this approach. It is not that I deny the divinity of Jesus, but *I too find great difficulty with this harsh and ruthless identification: Jesus = God.*" It is true that in connection not with this passage but with a passage on the Church from the same conversation Fr. Schillebeeckx assails the fidelity with which J. Spitz reported his words. In any event, the passage just cited (I forgot to say that the italics are mine) is quite likely not to have been misreported if we may judge by equivalent statements which Fr. Schillebeeckx himself published in 1966 (*Tijdschrift voor Theologie* 6 [1966] 276). I quote: "Since 1953 I have always been opposed to the formula: 'Jesus is God *and* [italics in the Dutch text.—Ed.] man' [*Remark:* But the Council of Chalcedon and later the third Council of Constantinople defined that "Jesus is truly God and truly man": *DS* 301 and 544], and also to the confusing expression: 'The man Jesus is God' [*Remark:* The Blessed Virgin is the mother of Christ insofar as Christ is a man, and the entire Church rightly addresses her as Mother of God]. . . . Such expressions as 'Jesus is not only man but also God' [*Remark:* There is nothing incorrect about such language] strip the incarnation of its deepest meaning." In the context of these strange criticisms Fr. Schillebeeckx proposes a different formulation of which he does approve: "Jesus, the Christ, is the Son of God *in humanity*" [italics by the author]. *Remark:* The formulation is unusual and rather obscure. Fortunately (or unfortunately) the author explains: "The deepest meaning of [revelation is, that (left out by Congregation,—Ed.)] God himself is revealed in humanity. The form in which God reveals himself (*Gods openbaringsgestalte*) is the man Jesus. The being of God manifests itself *in* [italics by the author] the humanity of Jesus." These explanations water down the meaning, and that is not surprising since the author means them to correct the impression given by such clear and firm formulations of the mystery as "Jesus is God and man."

Whatever may be said of the passage on Christology which J. Spitz puts into Fr. Schillebeeckx' mouth, it must be admitted that the—older—passage which I have just cited is in the same vein. Both distance themselves from the formulas which the Church has traditionally used in teaching the divinity of Jesus, and certainly have as their aim to weaken the meaning of these formulas. Consequently, though not in so many words, they resemble the texts cited earlier which assign a subsistence of its own to the humanity of Jesus.

f. The author accuses the questionnaire of an error in translation. He says that when he speaks of the humanity of Jesus he calls it a "personnlijk-menselijke zijnswijze" (B 543 in Dutch; 667 in English), an expression which the questionnaire translated as "manière d'être personnelle-humaine." This translation, he says, would require "persoonlijke-menselijke zijnswijze" in the original and comes down to attributing the person, the hypostasis, to the humanity itself of Jesus. In fact, however, he says, the translation should have read: "une manière d'être personnell*ement* humaine," the Dutch word "persoonlijk" without a final -e being an adverb, not an adjective. In his opinion, therefore, the expression no longer has the meaning which the questionnaire attributes to it. It simply means: a "formally spiritual" (R 78) human mode of existence. Let us not quibble about this final conclusion but simply accept it. But, as bad luck would have it, on the preceding page of his book (Dutch, 542; English, 665/6), the author himself describes the humanity of Jesus as a "menselijk-persoonlik*e* zijnswijze," an expression in which, contrary to the one just discussed, "menselijk" without a final -e becomes an adverb and "persoonlijke" with a final -e becomes an adjective. The certainly correct translation of this expression, in which the author is describing the humanity of Jesus, is "a humanly personal mode of being." Should not such a description of the *humanity* of Jesus mean that the latter is a hypostasis or person? This is even more true of this other expression which the author likewise applies to the *humanity* of Jesus: "een menselijke persoonswijze," a human mode of being a person (*ibid.*).

g. The author says further that in the fourth part of his book—the part with which the whole of my present section F is concerned—and with regard to *hypostatic identification,* (1) he does not make his own the expression "human person" because he judges it to be incorrect when taken in its ontological sense (R 76 and 77); (2) he uses this expression "human person" (B 667) only in order to "*deny* that Christ can be called a human person" (R 77; italics are Fr. Schillebeeckx').

I answer: in regard to (1): I have not reread the entire fourth part. However, I note that in it Fr. Schillebeeckx says on page 533 (English, 655) that "in his humanity which is constitutively relative to God the Father Jesus is rightly called in non-religious language a *human person* and in the language of faith the *Son of God*" [literal translation of the French; the French is incorrect.—Ed. (cf. English, 655): "What in non-religious language is called—and rightly called—a human person in the language of faith is called Son of God, by virtue of the constitutive relation of this human being to the Father"]. With regard to (2): It is not true that the author *denies* "that Christ can be called a human person." In the passage to which he refers, his very words are: "In the end we cannot (without all sorts of qualifications) describe him as simply and solely a 'human person,' for then there would indeed appear an inconceivable 'over against' between the man Jesus and the Son of God" (B 667). In good logic this also means: "In the end we can (with all sorts of qualifications, but not without them) describe him as a 'human person.'" The "all sorts of qualifications" are those required in order that despite the absence of anhypostasis (B 667) the humanity of Jesus may not be placed in an "over against" with regard to the Word (as it is with regard to the Father).

Let us conclude this section. In his notion of "some such thing as a 'hypostatic identification' without anhypostasis," Fr. Schillebeeckx does not simply abandon the divinity of Christ, but neither does he acknowledge this with the purity and fullness of meaning with which the Catholic Church professes it. He waters down this meaning.

He maintains that in Christ there is something like an identification (in fact, a supremely close union) between the hypostasis or person of the Word of God and the humanity of Jesus which does not lack a hypostasis of its own.

The Church for its part, in its understanding of Chalcedon and its interpretation of the New Testament, is not afraid to profess, without any restriction, that in Christ there is a single hypostasis or person, that of the Word, and two natures: the divinity and the humanity.

After this, Fr. Schillebeeckx and the Church alike assert that the humanity of Jesus is the supreme revelation of God. The difference is that the Church—unlike our author—does so without allowing itself to be *tempted* by a theology of a *more or less* Nestorian kind (Nestorian in the classical sense of the term, even if this be not a faithful reflection of "history"): a theology which posits two hypostases in Christ, that of his human reality (without anhypostasis) and that of the Word.

G. The mystery of the divine Trinity

The questionnaire says little about this great mystery. It has two reservations to make, but does not lay any great stress on them. "But let us not dwell on these points," it says. "The important thing here—now that in recent years some Catholic theologians have doubted or even denied the eternal existence of the Trinity in God—the really important thing is that you accept this existence without equivocation" (Q 49).

As for the two reservations, I shall mention only the one which Fr. Schillebeeckx takes up in his response. The questionnaire says: "You think that in God these persons are eternal and not contingent." To this there can evidently be no objection. But Fr. Schillebeeckx conceives the person of the Son, the Word (I shall say nothing here about the person of the Holy Spirit), as "the unique turning of the Father himself to *Jesus*" (B 658; italics mine). Consequently, in order to preserve the eternity and non-contingency of the divine Word, he must and does say: "God would be no God without creatures and Jesus of Nazareth" (668).

What reservation does the questionnaire have in this area? It says that there is a problem here which has "received the attention of the Church's magisterium . . . God and creation, cf., e.g., *DS* 3035." And this, it says, "you certainly cannot fail to see." In short, the questionnaire passes no judgment (Q 48 and 49).

Fr. Schillebeeckx explains that since creation and Jesus Christ exist, we know that (although these effects are *intrinsically contingent*) there is in God a "turning" to Jesus and the world which is creative *in God*, yet also, like everything *in God*, is *necessary in him* (R 88). I have already noted that in the "unique turning of the Father to Jesus" he recognizes the Word. He believes that he can thus reconcile the dogma of the intrinsic contingency of the world and Jesus with the necessity of the Word (and the Spirit) which, he thinks, inevitably implies creation.

This is to the point *if* the Church teaches only the intrinsic contingency of the created world and of Jesus, without also asserting that the latter are the result of *freedom* and of freedom of *choice*. But Vatican I teaches the following proposition in one of its canons: "If anyone maintains . . . that God created not by a will free of all necessity but by a necessity equal to that with which he loves himself . . ." (*DS* 3025). Does this teaching mean that the world is the result of a freedom of choice in God and not simply of an absence in him of antecedent necessity? This is certainly the common interpretation of the Council. To go any deeper into the matter, one would have to study the "Guntherian" doctrines which the Council is opposing. There is also the whole problem of tradition and St. Thomas (cf. *De pot.*, q. 1, a. 5).

The questionnaire is satisfied to mention the problem and the attention given to it by the magisterium. I see no basis for accusing it of excessive rigidity.

H. *The virginal conception and the mystery of the resurrection of Jesus*

1. *The virginal conception of Jesus.*—Fr. Schillebeeckx begins by offering his congratulations (R 89) that the questionnaire "has not failed to grasp the meaning of his text." His point, I take it, is that the questionnaire has rightly seen that he does not *deny* the *virginal conception* of Jesus.

This is true. The questionnaire does not say, however, as the author does in his Response (*ibid.*), that "*he says nothing either for or against this* profoundly authentic *tradition* of the Church." It points out, rather, that the author casts doubt on the biological aspect of the *virginal conception*, an aspect brought out in *Lumen gentium* (no. 62 [63, ed.]) by means of the phrase "*et quidem viri nescia.*" It seems to me that the questionnaire is correct. The objections (or rather some of them) are emphasized, the positive arguments are passed over in silence—and not a word is said to indicate that we are dealing here with a case in which, to a special degree, Scripture has to be read in the light of ecclesial tradition (B 554f, 600).

I do not think that the reasons which the author gives in his Response (89–90) are enough to justify his presentation of things—especially in the present-day theological crisis of which the author is certainly well aware.

2. *The resurrection of Jesus.*—In his Response Fr. Schillebeeckx begins by congratulating himself that the questionnaire admits (though my own impression is that it is not "admitting" but simply observing) that the author professes "the personal and bodily resurrection of Jesus" (R 83; B 645; Q 43). The questionnaire is critical of the fact that

without denying the discovery of the *empty tomb* Fr. Schillebeeckx avoids affirming it and that he has not attempted to assay the arguments to which many capable critics assign a high degree of importance. The author gives no answer to this criticism. Is the question one of faith? In any case I do not think it a purely historical and open question.

With regard to the appearances. The questionnaire is critical of the fact that in his book the author disputes them, even as psychological events. The questionnaire observes that the author speaks only of conversion experiences attributed to Jesus during his lifetime, and it indicates that this is not enough. Fr. Schillebeeckx answers by saying that the question is not one of faith. But is it a question unconnected with the faith? I would not say so. (The questionnaire points out that in a piece of writing which is subsequent to his great book Fr. Schillebeeckx allows that the grace of conversion which the disciples had experienced *may have* stimulated, *by way of consequence,* "some visual element." But "the concession made is minimal.")

The author says: "There were conversion models presented in the form of appearances, and . . . I see such models at work in the biblical accounts of the appearances" (R 84). This is an extreme critical position. It is not my task here to refute it on historical grounds, but I do not regard it as *simply an open question* from the standpoint of faith.

The author would like (*ibid.*) to have his readers agree that in his view (against Marxsen) faith in the resurrection is not simply a post-paschal interpretation of the pre-paschal life of Jesus. But the questionnaire says that this is precisely what the resurrection is for Fr. Schillebeeckx, for, it says, the author connects the apostles' faith in the resurrection with a conversion experience, or even an experience of presence. For it finds the author saying that the words of Jesus, "Where two or three are gathered in my name, there am I in the midst of them" (Mt 18:20), are "perhaps the purest, most adequate reflection of the Easter experience" (B 646; Q 44).

The author denies that "the visual elements [the appearances; but his version of these is by any accounting a watered down one] are the *foundation* of our faith in the resurrection." I grant, of course, that they are not the foundation of faith in the risen Jesus, but they do provide one of the many converging arguments, which differ in value for different individuals, that help to make our faith "reasonable," although this faith is not by any means a conclusion reached by reason.

The author thinks that the questionnaire (44) is wrong when it finds fault with him for not seeing that "the appearance narratives . . .

give expression in their own way to a *specific, 'foundational'* testimony." But is it not Fr. Schillebeeckx who reduces the specific and foundational character of the apostolic witness that arose out of the apostles' Easter experience, when he writes: "Despite the unrepeatable and peculiar status of the first apostles, who had known Jesus before his death, the way the apostles then found reason for 'becoming Christians' does not differ so very much in fundamentals from our way now" (B 647; cf. also 345–46)?

Finally, the questionnaire asks how even profound graces of conversion, unconnected with any mysterious appearances, can explain the fact that "the disciples were convinced not only that their Master lived on somehow in glory [in keeping with traditional ideas] but specifically that he had experienced a *resurrection* in the course of history, although it took him into the next world. The Jews," the questionnaire continues, "did not attribute such a resurrection to any of the patriarchs, to any of the ancient prophets or to any king; they did not think of attributing it even to the Messiah." All alike would have to await the general resurrection on the last day. Here, again, Fr. Schillebeeckx gives no answer.

Let me end this section.—The author's pages on the virginal conception of Jesus are disturbing to the reader.—His explanation of the resurrection of Jesus is good in that he accepts the personal and bodily resurrection of Jesus. It is inadequate from the standpoint of a sound exegesis (one that is historical, yes, but not hypercritical), especially since it casts doubt on the discovery of the empty tomb, and reduces the "appearances," at least in their substance, to conversion experiences which are attributed to the action of Jesus.[17]

---

17. The questionnaire speaks *briefly* about the Church, after observing that Fr. Schillebeeckx himself says *hardly anything* about it (Q 50). The author replies that he speaks of it constantly, but under such names as "Christian community" or "movement centered on Jesus." He takes this approach in order not to frighten off "marginal believers" who are allergic to the idea of Church, and because "ecclesiology will be the subject" of the third volume of his trilogy (R 90). However, the questionnaire cites a passage from an interview given by Fr. Schillebeeckx to J. Spitz, in which he speaks of the Church in very disturbing terms. But the author states (*ibid.*) that the passage from Spitz misrepresents his thinking. The interview was written by one who brought to it an attitude favorable to Fr. Schillebeeckx; I accept, however, that J. Spitz was incorrect. To what extent? I do not know. The author says, finally, that the questionnaire is guilty of a mistranslation. It translates *verbondenheid* (with Rome) as "sense of union"; according to the author, it should have translated the word as "affection." In my opinion, the word "affection" waters down the meaning of *verbondenheid*. It is of little importance, however, since he rejects Spitz' text.

A final word

In this evaluation of a response to a questionnaire there could be no question of passing judgment on the author's work, but only of examining where his answers provided all the desirable clarifications. The preceding pages have made it clear, I think, that sufficient light has not yet been thrown on a number of questions.

THE CONVERSATION
IN ROME

December 13–15, 1979

Introduction

Unlike the earlier states in the "investigation" of Schillebeeckx' orthodoxy the conversation in Rome was not much of a secret affair. The outside world was practically able to listen in on it via the two hundred journalists gathered in Rome. The "setting" of the conversation may therefore be presumed to be known; if need be, the reader can refresh his memory of it from Hebblethwaite's book, mentioned earlier.

The meetings in the "red chamber" of the Holy Office, however, were quite secret and, apart from Schillebeeckx' press conference afterward, they have continued to be secret down to the present. The meetings were, of course, no more of a "conversation" than the one to which, as I mentioned earlier, Hans Küng was invited, unless he had "now already" chosen to subscribe to the views of the Congregation. But Schillebeeckx was a considerably less contentious partner in conversation than his colleague from Tübingen. To be sure, he made some very obvious stipulations: information about the questioners, a counselor present with him. He did not even insist, however, on the use of his own native language or on inspection of the entire dossier, and when the stipulations he did make were rejected, he nonetheless did not refuse to take part in the conversations. Even when J. Galot—who for years had been sifting the "new Christology" for heresies and had in public only a few days before the event condemned Schillebeeckx' Christology, among others—turned out to be one of the questioners, Schillebeeckx limited himself to an official protest. In a published analysis mentioned earlier, B. van Iersel, who was finally allowed into a side room in order to be able to advise Schillebeeckx privately, has established that the meeting was really a trial. The record that follows here fully confirms this judgment.

Just before the meeting Schillebeeckx had been on sick-leave. In preparation for the conversation he went back to the earlier documents but quickly put them aside: the whole business seemed so unreal to him when compared with what he had had in mind when writing his book, and he did not expect a high-level academic discussion. He borrowed a copy of his book from an acquaintance in Rome.

The conversation was preceded by a visit to Cardinal Seper, Prefect of the Congregation. Seper thanked him for coming to Rome and now finally told him who would take part in the conversation on behalf of the Congregation: Msgr. Albert Descamps, former Rector of Louvain University and now Secretary of the Pontifical Biblical Commission, a professional exegete whose competence Schillebeeckx respected; Albert Patfoort, a fellow Dominican from French Flanders, a professor at the Dominican University in Rome, and a solid moderate Thomist; and Jean Galot, a professor at the Jesuit-run Gregorian University in Rome. When Schillebeeckx tried to protest against the presence of the last-named, Msgr. Hamer, the Secretary of the Congregation, quickly broke in and began to read an introductory statement on the status and purpose of the conversation. The conversation was to be "a stage in a process of clarification"; in addition to the book *Jesus*, Schillebeeckx' response to the questionnaire and his book *Interim Report* were to be introduced into the discussion; only what is objectively expressed in the texts, and not the subjective intention of the author, was to be discussed. The text of this introductory statement is given below.

When the conversation began (with Msgr. Alberto Bovone, Under-Secretary of the Congregation, in the chair), Schillebeeckx was given a number of sheets on which, under the headings communicated to him earlier, there was in each case a brief summary of the relevant issue and then a blank space. These papers, it became clear later on, were intended as preparation for the definitive minutes: in the empty space questions and answers were to be filled in. The other participants already had the questions written on their sheets, as Schillebeeckx quickly observed; he himself had to try to write them down quickly while they were being read to him. How this procedure worked can be seen from the fascimile given below of the two versions of the first sheet (Schillebeeckx' worksheet and the final version of the minutes). No wonder, then, that in the early part of the conversation (as he asked himself what the reason could be for this strange discrimination between himself and the other participants) he could hardly concentrate fully on the substance of the questions and gave nervous and sometimes confused answers, as he remembers it.

It should be noted that the minutes are not a real record nor were they intended to be (cf. the Conclusion of the minutes). The subjects were divided among the three questioners. Each of them could first give a general exposition and then present detailed questions, after which Schillebeeckx could formulate his answers, likewise in detail. Finally, in each case the essence of what had been said was dictated to the stenographers. In this way, a conversation of from seven to eight hours in length yielded a document that can comfortably be read in three-quarters of an hour. The end-result resembles a solid concentrate that becomes digestible only if water is added to it.

Schillebeeckx' answers in particular often seem to be *very* succinct. Especially striking is his repeated agreement with the main point being made in a question; the subsequent qualifications, which are no less essential in his view (especially his repeated insistence on the need of hermeneutical understanding), are less likely to catch the attention. The Congregation thus seems to win from him at last the concessions it had so long waited for (cf. especially at the beginning of the Evaluation, p. 96: "In it he makes almost no concession . . ."). In a conversation—certainly in *this* "conversation"—Schillebeeckx is at a disadvantage. As Van Iersel stressed in his study, we must not underestimate the pressure exerted by the entire "setting." It was only to Schillebeeckx that questions were being put, and for him a good deal was at stake.

Nevertheless the minutes also show that Schillebeeckx does not retreat from his basic position. Within a short compass we find his views on the value of religious language and concepts of faith and on the indispensable need of hermeneutics: "the immutable truth"—that ceremonial stallion of Roman theology—"is reached [only] *in* the hermeneutical translation" (A/e). Once again he explains the purpose of his book (e.g., B/c). And on questions concerned more with content he gives answers reminiscent of his Response.

On the final day, he and Van Iersel had an opportunity to check the minutes that had been drawn up. The session was not a very tranquil one for them (they did not know as yet whether a copy of the document would be given to them and so they tried to memorize as much of it as possible), but they proposed some emendations and these were ultimately accepted. Nonetheless a few points went wrong or else escaped Schillebeeckx' attention. (1) Only after a kind of ultimatum on Schillebeeckx' part was the status clarified of two remarks by "one of the experts" (in which this person, with little effort at nuancing his assertion, claims that Schillebeeckx is now saying something different than he had in his book): these are minority observations and not—as they were first presented—questions which Schillebeeckx had failed to answer (end of C and H).—(2) Next there arose a discussion (with regard to) a new issue (a discussion which the chairman rightly wanted to cut off but which Schillebeeckx himself allowed to continue "in order not to create frustration for one of the participants!"), in which the claim was made that there are indeed statements of faith which require no hermeneutic or explanation at all, e.g., "Jesus is God." Schillebeeckx objected that at least the word "God" needs explanation, because his colleague would surely not identify "God" with "Trinity" in this case, and yet "Trinity" is what God *is* according to the teaching of faith! This post-conversation discussion subsequently turned out to have been introduced into the minutes, again in a very succinct form, as the ending of B. Because this emendation was typed and not written, Schillebeeckx did not notice it in his final review and therefore did not check it.—(3) Only subsequently, again, did he notice that his answer to the question regarding Jesus' virginal conception (H) is recorded in much too apodictic a form. After the first sentence of his answer there should have been added: "But this also calls for hermenutical interpretation."—(4) And, finally, he did not notice that at the end of G it is said that he wants to add two points concerning the Eucharist, namely, a disclaimer of an interview and a clarification with regard to his "concelebration" with married priests, laity and women (!) in the critical community of Ijmond earlier that year. These, however, were not additions by Schillebeeckx himself but really answers given to questions put to him ("in parentheses" as it was said at the time). Later on he realized that he should have cut the questions short because they had nothing to do with his book and were therefore out of order. Even worse, however, is the fact that he is made to seem to offer a "confession" on his own initiative and this in a manner reminiscent of a Russian party congress.

A somewhat more humorous episode has not been recorded as such in the minutes, namely, the end of a misunderstanding regarding the historical value which Schillebeeckx attributes to the words of eucharistic institution. In answer to the first question under this heading (G/a) he now referred the questioner to the correct page of his book; the questioner, very much surprised, saw that Schillebeeckx was right. After the vain search made by the anonymous author of the third document (the Evaluation), the questioner could naturally not have expected this.

At the beginning of these meetings Schillebeeckx had made an official protest against a number of aspects of the whole procedure: the presence of Galot, given his previous condemnation of Schillebeeckx; the withholding of the names of the three questioners; the failure to put the questions on the sheets given to him; the fact that in the early stages he did not know the name of his own "defender" and thus did not know whether the latter had represented him correctly; the rejection of Van Iersel as his official "counselor"; the decision to be made at "a higher level" by persons who had not themselves seen or heard him.

The protest was simply noted.

THE CONVERSATION

Introduction to the Conversation.
Read to Fr. Schillebeeckx on December 13, 1979 in the presence of the Cardinal Prefect

I thank you, Reverend Father, for agreeing to take part in the meeting that is now beginning. I think it necessary to define its purpose and spirit.

These conversations are being held within the framework of the mission that has been entrusted to our Congregation by the Apostolic Constitution *Regimini Ecclesiae Universae* according to which the Congregation for the Doctrine of the Faith "has the task of safeguarding the doctrine about faith and morality throughout the entire Catholic world" (III, ch. I, no. 1).

We have carried out this mission in accordance with the prescriptions of our *Agendi ratio in doctrinarum examine* (January 15, 1971). It was within this framework that a letter of "protest" ("contestatio") was addressed to you on October 20, 1976, to which you kindly gave an answer that reached here on April 26, 1977. The present meeting has its place within that same framework.

Our purpose here is the kind of "conversation" for which provision is made in articles 13–15 of the *Agendi ratio*. I think it worthwhile to cite these in so many words: "(13) Statements made which are regarded as erroneous or dangerous are to be pointed out to the author who, within one month of available time, may communicate his answer in writing. If there is also need of a conversation, the author will be invited to meet and confer with men appointed by the Sacred Congregation.—(14) These appointed individuals must make at least a summary written record of the conversation and, along with the author, sign the pages containing it.—(15) Both the written response of the author and the summary of the conversation, if any such have

116

been held, will be submitted to an Ordinary Congregation so that it may decide on the matter. But if the written response of the author or the summary of the conversation brings to light new points of doctrine which need to be examined more carefully, the response or the summary of the conversation is first to be referred to a board of consultors."

These articles yield the following conclusions with respect to the present meeting.

1. The discussion has to do with doctrinal positions as these find expression in the objective order; it is not concerned with subjective intentions and the internal forum.

2. The participants are not here in order to pass judgment or make decisions but to supply fuller information to those whose function it is to pass judgment and make decisions, namely, the member Cardinals of this Congregation and, in the last resort, the Sovereign Pontiff himself.

3. The questions to be asked of you will deal with points communicated to you in connection with your book *Jesus: An Experiment in Christology* and with a few further matters suggested by your subsequent book, *Interim Report*. These questions take into account the written response you have already given and are asked for purposes of clarification and not with any polemical intent.

4. Your answers to these questions will be taken down in writing; the written version will be submitted to you for your approval and so that you may request corrections. Once signed by you and the authorized delegates of the Congregation, this set of responses will be the only authentic text of the conversation. It is the one that will be passed on for examination by the Cardinals of this Congregation and then communicated to the Holy Father.

Let me say also how much we hope that discretion will be exercised with regard to the content of this meeting. All those who take part in it in the name of the Congregation are, in any case, bound to a strict observance of pontifical secrecy (cf. Instruction of February 4, 1974, art. 1, par. 3).

I shall end by noting that attention ought not to be focused solely on the necessarily technical aspect of this "conversation." The meeting is meant to be a stage in a process of clarification; I very much hope, therefore, that it will be marked by an ecclesial spirit of mutual respect and trust and that it will help to eliminate the ambiguities and misunderstandings which have appeared and manifested themselves in public opinion about your case.

✠ *J. Hamer*

CONVERSATION

Between the Sacred Congregation for the Doctrine of the Faith and Reverend Father Edward Schillebeeckx December 13–15, 1979

A. *The extent of revealed truth, the content of faith, and the meaning of Christian salvation*

It seems from what you say in your writings that the whole essence of the Christian message can be summed up as salvation coming from God in the man Jesus: "One is already a *Christian* in entertaining [this 'first-order assertion'], even though at the level of 'second-order assertions' a whole range of nicer distinctions and definitions may exist" and "even though those who accept this may adopt different positions on what the fullness of Jesus Christ entails" (*Jesus,* 549 and 30; italics in the Dutch original).

Everything else would then be interpretation and formulation, which on the one hand would have to be thrown out of court if it claimed to be a complete expression of the message, "an all-embracing, theoretical 'Christological system'" (79; cf. 423 and 669) and which, on the other hand, would be relative to a particular culture and could not therefore serve as a "final criterion" (22), inasmuch as, according to you, we as Christians are not bound by all these "interpretative elements" (*Interim Report* [*on the Books Jesus and Christ* (New York, 1981)], 15) or, as you put it in *Christ* [: *The Experience of Jesus as Lord* (New York, 1980)], by all "that old conceptuality."

Q(uestion)—a. In your view, is it enough, for Catholic faith, to believe that salvation comes to us from God in the man Jesus?

A(nswer)—to a. The term "enough" calls for a distinction. It must be understood here in the context of the minimum required in order to be a Christian. I may remind you at this point that my book is addressed primarily to non-believers and marginal Christians. It is clear that, as far as I am concerned, this is not the normal condition of faith.

Q—b. Does faith not include other statements which cannot be deduced from the one mentioned and which must be maintained as expressing revealed truth?

A—to b. Faith certainly does include other affirmations which are either preambles to faith or flow from faith and which must be accepted if one is not to set oneself in contradiction to faith in the salvation that comes in Jesus Christ.

Q—c. You are certainly correct in thinking that no doctrinal formula or set of formulas can express the mystery in its totality, with all its virtualities and all its concrete aspects, present and future. But do you really think that such a claim has ever been made in Christian teaching? Do you know of examples of such a claim? If there are no such claims, is it possible to hold that more detailed statements regarding the mysteries will only improverish the latter (*Jesus*, 323 [should be: p. 650—Ed.])?

A—to c. In my opinion, which I formulate here in passing, there are theological systems which have had an essentialist orientation and have set too much store by conceptual expression. But I do not think that this is the case with the magisterium. Furthermore, when I use the word "impoverish" I mean it in the general sense that every conceptual definition represents an impoverishment by comparison with Christian theological experience; but at the same time it is an authentic specification that sheds light on the profound meaning of the mystery.

Q—d/1. Do you not think it possible to express in an exact, although analogical way, that is, not univocally but also not equivocally, specific aspects of the real mystery of God, of Christ, of salvation?

A—to d/1. Yes, I do think it possible. I prefer to say "in a true way" rather than "in an exact way." I reject the adjective "exact" because it seems to say that the mystery is "captured" in abstract conceptual knowledge of it whereas in fact it is only "sighted" through the concept.

Q—d/2. Do you not think that this is what was intended in the formulas of faith, and this with the real purpose of teaching, of saying what is?

A—to d/2. I am in agreement on this point.

Q—d/3. Do you not think that the meaning, the content of these formulas can be permanently true, that it can be communicated through faithful translation of the formulas, and that in formulations that may have undergone variation the content set forth can remain and has in fact remained completely homogeneous (*secum constans*) (*Mysterium Ecclesiae* 5, 2 and 3)?

A—to d/3. With regard to this point I note that "true" and "permanently true" are synonyms. Here however the hermeneutical problem arises. The Chalcedonian formulation, for example, is "permanently true," but the meaning of the formulas themselves has changed. It is necessary, therefore, that what is "permanently true" in the context of Chalcedon be understood in the light of that same context. Now in modern culture the words used by Chalcedon have taken on a different meaning. If then we want to be faithful to the true statement of Chalcedon we must retranslate what is being said into a modern vocabulary. The content of the statements of Chalcedon can be determined; it must be retranslated for the people of our time and at the same time remain "permanently true" in this faithful and homogeneous translation.

Q—e. The Dogmatic Constitution *Dei Verbum*, no. 11, 2, states that everything (really!) affirmed by the inspired authors must be regarded as affirmed by the Holy Spirit. Do you think you can say that this is not normative for us as a word coming directly from God, normative according to its (real) literal meaning (*Jesus*, 57) and that it does not constitute so many eternal truths which are immutable, not indeed in the letter of the words expressing them but in the precise content that is transmitted through the words, and which in fact only need to be hermeneutically translated for our time (cf. *Jesus*, 59–60)?

A—to e. Yes, I accept these statements. I simply emphasize the point that the last two terms (immutable truths and their hermeneutical translation) must be taken together. What I do not accept is the idea that there is an immutable truth which can be determined *in itself*. The immutable truth is reached *in* the hermeneutical translation, the interpretation by the Church. The subject of this hermeneutical activity is actually the Church and therefore the magisterium; theologians also make their contribution to it, their "specialized service," so to speak.

B. The normative character (for faith and theology) of the ecumenical councils and the infallible teaching of the Popes

You write: "Nor indeed can the faith of the Christian be identified completely with even the most official articulations of it, although the mystery of faith which they enshrine is validly and truly expressed in them" (*Jesus,* 49), and you add in *Interim Report:* "This liturgical mysticism [of Christ] found an appropriate expression in Nicea and Chalcedon, albeit in terms of the conceptuality of the later period of the ancient world *(laat-antiek begrippelijke expressie)* (143). Again in *Interim Report,* you say: "I have . . . decided not to go into criticisms which . . . in fact identify true Christianity or orthodoxy with the Roman-Hellenistic way in which it has been expressed, so that in the last resort Greek philosophy becomes the criterion by which interpretations of faith are judged" (143, n. 1).

On the other hand, you say: "I have set out to search for 'meta-dogmatic' clues, that is, through and beyond ecclesiastical dogma . . . and to pursue them without knowing in advance where this would take me" (*Jesus,* 34), and you say twice that "the starting point for any (modern) Christology or Christian interpretation of Jesus is not simply Jesus of Nazareth, still less the Church's *kerygma* or creed" (*Jesus,* 44 and 56).

Remark inserted by Fr. E. Schillebeeckx: I call attention, right at the beginning, to the fact that the ideas just summed up here do not constitute a definitive principle and must be seen within my overall plan, which is to provide a *manuductio* of an "apologetic" kind.

Q—a. Do you regard that which has been defined by the ecumenical councils as a truth of faith (transcending all human philosophy)?

A—to a. Yes, I do, but I think a distinction is needed. There are dogmatic formulas which are expressed in a "common sense" philosophy; other formulations, however, can only be understood in terms of a particular philosophical context (for example, Hellenistic philosophy for the Trinitarian and Christological formulations). But the content of these formulas can be discovered by later generations; it requires, however, a hermeneutical interpretation, especially at times of great cultural change.

Q—b. Do you think that what has been defined in infallible papal statements must be accepted as an affirmation of faith?

R—to b. Certainly, but the hermeneutical problem always arises. For every dogma which the Church defines in an act of infallible teaching remains located in history. In addition, the question arises of the degree to which one is able to grasp the content of a dogmatic formula through its conceptual formulation. And this development continues without a break.

Q—c. Do you think that when a theologian applies himself to an historical or exegetical investigation, he cannot sincerely regard himself as having to leave aside the affirmations of faith that have been made by the Catholic Church or seriously consider a datum of faith as a "hypothesis" which he "must verify (or disallow)" (*Jesus*, 617)?

A—to c. I grant the point. But I remind you that my method is one of apologetic *manuductio*. Acting as an historian, I think that at that level the question must be left open. What is involved is a methodical, not a theoretical doubt. I apply this methodical doubt in order to establish with regard to Jesus a minimum that is not open to scientific attack. And I believe that this minimum is solid enough to make possible a first confrontation of non-believers or marginal believers with the message of Christ and the faith of the Church.

Q—d. Do you not think that in the judgments he really makes about things as they are a theologian must adopt as the supreme norm of his thinking not his own conception of the Jesus of history but the thought of the Church about Jesus?

A—to d. I admit that is entirely the case for a dogmatic theologian.

Q—e. For example, can a theologian evade the question "Is Jesus God?" and not answer either Yes or No on the grounds that the expression "to be God" calls for a hermeneutic?

A—to e. No, he cannot evade this question. He must answer either Yes or No. But the statement "Jesus is God" must be immediately spelled out [e.g.] in the affirmation of faith that he is the *Son of God*, the incarnated second Person of the Trinity.

C. Jesus-God, Jesus Son of God, a pre-existent person who has become man

You write: "In his humanity Jesus . . . is defined by his relationship to God. In other words: the deepest nature of Jesus lay in his personal relationship with God." In order to define the nature of this relationship more closely, you make reference to the eschatological prophet who speaks face to face with God as a man does with his friend. You also say that the difference between Jesus and other human beings is not that he is God but rather that "as a man in his full humanity Jesus can only be defined in terms of his unique relationship with God and man (this, too, was a well-known aspect of the eschatological prophet)" (*Interim Report*, 141). You offer still other clarifications: "God belongs . . . to the definition of the man Jesus" because of the relationship between the man Jesus and God *(ibid.)*. "God is greater even than his supreme, decisive and definitive self-revelation in the man Jesus" *(ibid.)*. "In Jesus God reveals his own being by willing to be in *him* salvation for humanity" *(ibid.*, 142). You add that you cannot be more precise; this seems to mean that you refuse to say in your Christology what has been explicitly said by the Councils of Nicea and Chalcedon.

Q—Is Jesus for you the divine person of the pre-existing Son, who became man and in whom there are two natures, one divine and the other human?

A—I accept what the Council of Chalcedon says about the truth of Jesus: "true God and true man," "one and the same" (i.e., a totality). I therefore accept the divinity of Jesus, and as a dogmatic theologian I never say that Jesus is a human person. But, because my intention is to explain the divinity of Jesus to people of our day, who unless they are theologians, do not understand excessively subtle theological expressions, I avoid using the Chalcedonian formula, even while explaining it in a way I think homogeneous and faithful. It is in this sense that I say that Jesus is "humanly a person," which does not mean that the man Jesus has a human person. Or again, I speak of a "personalist humanity." In his "personalist humanity" Jesus is the Son of God and thus the second person of the Trinity. I proceed in this way because though I accept the hypostatic union I prefer to avoid the anhypostasis implied in neo-Chalcedonianism, for (taken in the *modern* sense of the word, which is different from the ancient sense) anhypostasis implies a loss of human fullness in Jesus; it means (when taken in this modern sense) that Jesus would not be "true man." This is why I use the words "personalist humanity" and "identification."

When I say that Jesus called God his "Creator," I think this is implied in, for example, the Our Father. And by "God" here I mean the Father. My intention is not to say that the person of the Son was created, but only the humanity of Jesus.

One of the experts made the following observation:
With regard to the answer given to this question, namely, the affirmation of the divine person of the pre-existing Son who became man: this does not seem to me to be in harmony with the more usual presentation of the person of Jesus that is to be found in *Jesus, Christ* and *Interim Report*. In these books Jesus is presented as a human being with a unique relationship to God; when a distinction is made between God and human beings, he is on the side of human beings, and when the question arises of whether or not he is God, your answer is not that he is God but rather that he is a man who is defined by his unique relationship with God (cf. the Epilogue of *Interim Report*). Moreover, you depart not only from the formula of Chalcedon (one person and two natures) but also from its meaning: with regard to the two natures you say: "We can never speak of two components: humanity *and* divinity, only of two total 'aspects' " (*Jesus* 655), because it is in the humanity that Jesus' being of God, being of the Father, is realized. With regard to the unity of person, you propose a hypostatic identification, an identity between a personally human mode of being and a personally divine mode of being (667). Such an identity is contradictory.

Fr. Schillebeeckx answered that this is a personal opinion and that the expert has the right to propose it.

D. Salvific value of the sacrifice of Christ

You write that salvation coming from God is not to be identified with the passion and death of Jesus (*Jesus*, 651). In *Christ* you explain this teaching more fully: God does not will the suffering of human beings, and the Christian message contains no explanation of evil or of the history of our suffering. The statement that God required the death of Jesus as compensation for our sins is blasphemous; it springs from a sadistic mystic of suffering that is alien to the most authentic tendencies of the great Christian tradition (*Christ*, 728).

Man is saved by Jesus "despite his death"; the expression "despite his death" says too little, but is to be understood as meaning that God intended to overcome death through the resurrection of Jesus from the dead (*ibid.*, 729).

Q—Do you think that Jesus saved the human race by the expiatory sacrifice of the cross, or in other words that he saved it not despite his suffering and death but by means of his suffering and death?

A—My answer is Yes. I said so in my book *Christ* and in the article entitled "I believe in Jesus of Nazareth: The Christ, the Son of God, the Lord" [Dutch: "Ik geloof in Jezus van Nazareth," *Tijdschrift voor geestelijke Leven*, 35 (1979) 461–462; English version in: *Journal of Ecumenical Studies* 17 (1980) No. 1, 25]: "Jesus' death is suffering-by-and-for-others as the crown of an unconditional praxis of right doing and of opposition to evil and suffering."

The sacrifice of Jesus expiates our sins.

The death of Jesus has, as such, a salvific value. But I wish also to stress the point that the death must not be isolated from the human life of Jesus, thus turning it into a barren kerygma. We must unify the life, death and resurrection of Christ.

The expression "despite his death" means: Despite the execution which was the doing of men—Jews and Romans—God has not been checkmated by this occurrence. He took this historical fact into his plan of salvation.

The expression "blasphemous[ly] claim" refers only to caricatures of St. Anselm's theory, such as may be found even today in certain statements made, for example, in preaching and catechesis.

Q—Your answer does not explain the silence of the book (1) on God's will with regard to the death of Jesus, and (2) on the expiatory nature of this death.

A—I developed these points in *Jesus*, 225–41, especially 238ff, and in other writings.

E. Jesus' consciousness of being Messiah and Son of God Messiahship

In your book (*Jesus*, 105–397) you discuss various aspects of the ministry of Jesus. Thus you write (140) that the focus of Jesus' message is this "cheering news": "God's lordly rule is at hand." You explain (141–42) that "God's lordship . . . is the exercise of his peculiar and divine function as sovereign Creator."

In the course of your discussion you emphasize various kinds of *dicta et gesta Jesu* (words and deeds of Jesus), many of which bring out clearly the "originality" of Jesus. Thus you explain that the Beatitudes represent an "eschatological revolution" (172), especially because of the fact that all human weakness is even now being overcome by the coming of the reign of God (171–78) and the fact that, since God is love, he now restores hope to those who weep (*ibid.*).

Further on, you speak of the "beneficence" which Jesus practiced (179–200), especially for the purpose of rousing human beings to an "unconditional faith in God" (199). You speak of Jesus inaugurating a time of joy, marked by the "impossibility of fasting" (201–6). You say that by "meal-sharing in fellowship, whether with notorius 'tax collectors and sinners' or with his friends, casual or close . . . Jesus shows himself to be God's eschatological messenger" (218) and that this fellowship is "an offer here and now of eschatological salvation" (*ibid.*) [the French replaces the final two words with "divine benefits"— Ed.]. You write that Jesus "exposes this ideology [of the law]" (256), especially because it "had established an ethic as an independent screen between God and man" (*ibid.*).

Q—a. Do you mean, by these various statements, to exclude the historical likelihood that the titles "Son of God" and "Messiah" were applied to Jesus?

A—to a. No. I leave the question open at the historical level. But I have given a positive answer in my little book [*Interim Report*].

I think that Jesus was conscious of being the Messiah, but the Messiah in the sense of the messianic eschatological prophet. If I have made little use of the term "Messiah" when speaking of him, it is in order to avoid using it as implying that Jesus was a political and revolutionary Messiah. On the other hand, I give a very full meaning to the expression "*the* eschatological prophet."

Jesus' Sonship

You write (*Jesus*, 258): "The distinctive relation of Jesus to God was expressed in the primitive Christian churches more especially by use of the honorific title 'Son of God' and 'the Son.' These were *Christian* identifications of Jesus of Nazareth after his death. Jesus never spoke of himself as 'the Son' or 'Son of God'; there is no passage in the Synoptics pointing in this direction" (italics in the Dutch original).

You write: "What is certain is that he referred in a special way to God as *Abba*" (258; cf. 258–60). But you add that the correlative title "the Son," "as applied by Jesus to himself, can nowhere be demonstrated (by the critical method) from the New Testament" (261).

Q—b. Do you in the same way exclude the possibility that the title "the Son" was to be found on the lips of Jesus himself?

A—to b. Again, no. At the historical level I leave the question open. I think that in the relation of Jesus to the Father there is implied the consciousness of being the only Son, and this even if he himself never used the term "the Son."

I realize that the passage quoted (from p. 258 of my book) is a little too apodictic. But I have softened it in *Christ* to this effect: that since we find so many "logia" referring to the Father, this implies the importance of the correlative term "Son." I can also accept that Jesus was in fact addressed by the messianic title "Son of God."

F. Jesus and the foundation of the Church

You speak of the consciousness Jesus had that the coming of the Kingdom was imminent; you leave open the question of whether this was a mistake on his part (152), but your view is that there is hardly any room for denying that he expected the final events to come soon (177).

You think that the New Testament texts on the Church are secondary; what Jesus really did will was the salvation of Israel, all Israel (146). This, it seems, did not include willing the Church; besides, how could he have willed it if the events of the end-time were at hand?

The question therefore arises: in your view, did Jesus intend to found the Church?

A—I must say that this point surprises me somewhat. After all, I say very little about this subject in my book, since I intend to develop the ecclesiological implications in a third volume.

But as far as I am concerned, it is clear that Jesus intended to found the Church and that this foundation, which took explicit and formal shape on Pentecost, is an extension of the choice of the Twelve as representatives of the twelve tribes of Israel.

In addition, when I say that when Jesus looked for the events of the end to come soon, I mean by this that he was conscious of the proximity of the eschatological Kingdom and not of an apocalyptic consummation (after the manner of John the Baptist, for example). The proper context for Jesus is eschatology, not apocalyptic.

G. Jesus and the institution of the Eucharist

You write (*Jesus,* 308) that in the texts of institution the most recent stratum is made up of liturgical formulas that were current in the Church (*kerkelijk-liturgische formules*).

Q—a. On the assumption that the texts of institution as we now find them are liturgical formulas, do you think that they also inform us of what Jesus said at the Supper?

A—to a. Yes, in substance, as I say in *Jesus,* 307, because the Eucharist is a historical anamnesis of what happened at the Last Supper.

With regard to these same formulas you say that "the post-Easter character of the texts of institution is clear" (literal translation of Dutch, 253; cf. English, 308).

Q—b. When you say that "the post-Easter character of the texts of institution is clear," do you mean to say that their origin is entirely post-Easter?

A—to b. I say that the origin of these words and of the Eucharist in its entirety is to be found in the Last Supper and in what Jesus said and did at the Last Supper. I do not give a more extended explanation in the book *Jesus* because the emphasis here is different: my purpose is to bring to light the consciousness Jesus had of the salvific value of his death. This also explains why I do not speak here of 1 Cor 11: I am not discussing the Eucharist as such; on the other hand I think I did this in an earlier little book entitled *The Eucharist* [New York, 1968].

You say (308) that the logion in Mk 14:25; Lk 22:18 represents "an older vein which according to F. Hahn belongs 'to the primeval rock of the tradition.' " But you add that even here we see in the second half of the verse ("until that day when I drink it new in the Kingdom of God") the post-Easter mark of the Church.

Q—c. You say of Mk 14:25 = Lk 22:18 that it is an older *logion*, but you add that even here there are secondary elements. How are we to understand these "secondary" elements?

A—to c. I refer to page 308 [Dutch, 253] of *Jesus* where the text admittedly gives the impression that the second part of the *logion* is secondary. I grant that this way of putting it is unfortunate. I correct it, however (308; Dutch, 254), by explaining that what is secondary is the combining of the two parts of the *logion*. I consider both parts to be in fact *ipsissima verba*. I have developed this point further in *Interim Report*.

Q—d. If in a discussion of the Eucharist one takes the historically legitimate approach of calling in question the *strictly* passover character of the farewell meal, does not a certain danger in the application of methodical doubt manifest itself? In other words: If the Supper really is a passover meal, does one not impoverish it by hypothesizing that it is not?

A—to d. I agree; but I repeat that I am not here engaging in a dogmatic explanation of the Eucharist. My point of view differs from that of dogmatic theology. I am adopting here the perspective of the historian or, if the term be preferred, of the apologetic theologian. From the standpoint of dogmatic theology I fully accept the passover character of the Supper.

I add two clarifications with regard to the Eucharist. First, I do not acknowledge as accurate the answer published in the interview in *Il Regno*. As a matter of fact I did say that Jesus instituted the Eucharist. Unfortunately, the way in which statements made in an interview are reproduced is too often defective. I also wish to deny that I have taken part in a concelebration with married priests and with laypersons, women among them, although newspapers have said I did. At this ceremony only one priest—married, it is true—celebrated;

some of the participants were simply asked to stand in a circle around the altar. I explained the facts of this matter to the Socius of the Master General of my Order. I must also say that I have had occasion to protest against priests not using the precise phrases of institution when they celebrate the Eucharist.

H. Virginal conception of Jesus

You write that the virginal birth, narrated in Matthew 1:18–20 and Luke 1:26–38, does not come from historical information but from theological reflection. It signifies that the conception or birth of Jesus is from God (*vanuit God*), as a being filled with the Spirit of God (*Gedstesvervulling*). But it was increasingly understood in a biological and material sense (554). The account is a Christological interpretation according to which "Jesus is holy and Son of God from the very first moment of his human existence" (555).

Q—Whence the question: Do you consider the virginal conception of Jesus to be a truth of faith: a virginal conception understood in the corporeal sense as it is meant in the traditional statement that Jesus was conceived of the Virgin Mary by the power of the Holy Spirit?

A—I accept this, and I believe it in virtue of the magisterium of the Church which has spoken on this point. But this truth of faith regarding the virgin birth is not the object of my study in *Jesus*, 554–55, where my purpose is quite different, namely, to do Christology, not Mariology.

An expert observed here that the answer given is a good one but that the text itself gives the impression that the birth of Jesus is not virginal in the bodily sense and that the story rather represents a Christological interpretation according to which Jesus is holy, Son of God from his very birth.

I. Objective reality of the resurrection of Christ

a. The empty tomb

You write that in the story of the empty tomb (Mk 16:1–8) "the style of an 'angelophany' . . . serves to inform the reader that the apostolic faith in the crucified-and-risen One is a *revelation by God* to the Church" (334; italics in the Dutch original).

With regard to the burial of Jesus (a subject connected with the preceding) you express yourself with great brevity, saying that the fact "is difficult to place, historically speaking" (347) and that the story may be "a Christian legend" (*ibid.*).

Q—In your view, can this pericope (Mk 16:1–8) nonetheless teach or inform us about "what happened at the tomb" shortly after the death of Jesus?

A—On this point my thinking has progressed between *Jesus* and *Interim Report*. In *Jesus* I did not make enough of a connection between the empty tomb and the resurrection. I realized subsequently that for the authors of the New Testament the link was a closer one than I had thought at first. In this sense, the discovery of the empty tomb is perhaps a sign that mediates faith. I assert only that our faith in the resurrection cannot be based *solely* on the sign of the empty tomb. I am reacting here against a certain empiricism in the way the sign of the empty tomb is treated.

With regard to the mention of the burial: I must acknowledge that I said nothing about it in *Jesus* because, while it is important as evidence of the real death of Jesus, it was less important for my purpose, which was to follow the journey of the disciples to the Easter faith. There was no special motive for the omission.

With regard to Mark 16:8, I admit that the possibility must be left open of a lost ending which speaks of Christophanies in Galilee.

b. *The appearances*

Q—b/1. You say that the "Q community" does not know of appearances, and you observe that there is the same silence on the part of St. Paul in 1 Thessalonians 1:10; 4:14 and 1 Corinthians 15:3–5. Does this mean that in your view the appearances are a thematization found in some Churches and not in others, a thematization which would be rather late?

A—to b/1. I say in *Jesus* that I see some local churches which do not know the appearance theme. I also note that the situation is quite different for the "Q tradition" than for 1 Thessalonians and 1 Corinthians, since in the case of the latter we have other texts of St. Paul which prohibit us from concluding that he was ignorant of the appearance theme. For the "Q tradition," on the other hand, we have no parallels, and I must grant that the position I take on this point is hypothetical.

In any case, this is the most hypothetical part of my entire book. Although I regard the hypothesis of the "Q community" as a serious one, I am not unaware of the doubts that exist concerning it. My intention is simply to say that the faith of the community in the resurrection is not based solely on the sign of the empty tomb and the appearances. But I have also explained, in additions introduced into my book [the third edition of the Dutch version to be found in all translations], that in the New Testament there is an intrinsic connection between appearances and resurrection.

On the other hand, I do not say that the thematization of the appearances is late; I say that it was known only in some ecclesial communities and unknown in others. These latter, however, accepted it, once they encountered it, as being fully in accord with the kerygma. But, I repeat, I grant that this is a hypothesis. And my intention is not to overvalue the "Q source" in order to minimize the resurrection.

Q—b/2. Do you not seem to exclude the mediation of the appearances?

A—to b/2. I do not exclude this mediation, but I do say that the appearance stories thematize a real post-Easter experience. I admit the historicity of the appearances, but the appearances as such are not the formal basis of our faith in the resurrection. That is why I expressly bring in the other mediations: in order to have a broader basis.

Q—b/3. With regard to the various Pauline texts on his Damascus experience, you seem to exclude an experience involving a vision, especially in *Jesus*, 361. How, then, should we understand the Damascus experience?

A—to b/3. I do not deny the reality of the Damascus experience. I say only that the sensible repercussion in the form of visual elements, among which the vision as such belongs, is secondary in my view. The most important thing in the experience of the risen Jesus is the cognitive element, and this is what I emphasize. I think that, given this element, we have everything that is essential in the Damascus vision and in the appearances generally.

Q—b/4. With regard to the final pericopes in the Gospels (pericopes that are late in their present form), do you not think that they have a "pre-history" in Christian tradition?

A—to b/4. Yes. Their ecclesial character is obvious, but they certainly are based on a very old tradition.

Q—b/5. All things considered, do you not think that a strict faith in the resurrection is *very* old in the primitive community and that at a very early date it appealed for support to the testimony of the women regarding the empty tomb and of the beneficiaries of the various Christophanies?

A—to b/5. I admit that this tradition was present from the very beginning. In my book I say only that this was true of some communities but not of all.

Q—b/6. It seems that the view you express is this: conviction about the resurrection comes from a faith experience, an experience of conversion to the pneumatic presence of Christ, and it is this experience that occasions a certain visualization in the form of appearances. But the testimony of the Gospels moves rather in the opposite direction, for it shows us how conviction regarding the resurrection arose out of the appearances; it was the appearances of the risen Christ that led to the disciples' faith in the resurrection, a faith which was often not readily elicited. This divergence between the interpretation you give and the testimony of the Gospels seems a rather serious matter, given the importance of the objective foundation of faith in the resurrection, a foundation which we find the Gospels supplying by means of the appearance stories.

A—to b/6. On the one hand, I grant that the emphasis is different in my presentation as compared with the letter of the New Testament. But, on the other hand, I deny any real difference, since in substance I am saying the same thing when I accentuate the cognitive element in the post-Easter experience. And it is this cognitive element that provides us with the objective but non-empiricist basis for our faith in the resurrection of Christ.

*   *   *

This document is the report of the conversation which took place at the offices of the Congregation for the Doctrine of the Faith on December 13 and 14, 1979, between Reverend Father Edward Schillebeeckx, O.P., on the one side, and, on the other, His Excellency Msgr. Albert L. Descamps, Reverend Father Albert Patfoort, O.P., and Reverend Father Jean Galot, S.J., who were delegated for the purpose by the same Congregation. The meeting was chaired by Msgr. Alberto Bovone, Under-Secretary of the Congregation.

The report reflects the norms established by the *Agendi ratio in doctrinarum examine* of January 15, 1971, articles 13 to 15. That is: (1) it states the *main points* ("summatim," cf. art. 14) of the conservation about the nine points determined in advance, and this in the form of an introduction and a summary presentation of the questions and answers; the detailed content of the exchanges is not given verbatim; (2) from the standpoint of content it records the *clarifications* regarding the said nine points which were requested by the delegates of the Congregation and in its name and given by Reverend Father Schillebeeckx; these clarifications were required in view of the judgment to be passed; (3) it is to be placed in the dossier that will be examined later on by the competent authorities, who are, in the first instance, the member Cardinals of the Congregation.

Rome, December 15, 1979   [signed by:]   *A. Bovone*
                                                    E. Schillebeeckx
                                                           J. Galot
                                                       A. Patfoort
                                                      A. Descamps

CONCLUSIONS

November 20, 1980

Introduction

At the final meeting in Rome, Msgr. J. Hamer, Secretary to the Congregation for the Doctrine of the Faith, let it be understood that it might well be some time before a statement on Schillebeeckx' orthodoxy would reach him. In fact it took the Congregation nearly a year before it managed to agree on a (provisional) conclusion. By our present day standards of justice this is an intolerably long time to wait, especially since the accused had meanwhile received not a single hint from Rome—except, of course, for the condemnation of Hans Küng, and this had occurred only a few days after the "conversation." The only excuse the Secretary offered for this delay was that Rome takes its time about everything, which, apparently, one is expected to consider a sufficient reason. As a matter of fact, the delay follows the same rhythm as the entire procedure up to this point. Between each of its stages more than a year elapsed, except between the original questionnaire and Schillebeeckx' response, but, then, the latter probably wasn't all that busy.

All the more reason, perhaps, to expect an extensive and solid document as the outcome of an investigation of such length. In a letter Schillebeeckx received at the end of November 1980 Cardinal Seper himself described extensively the various documents produced in more than four years; and, of course, the Cardinal could have added that a good deal of work had been done, in secret, even before the first questionnaire was composed. The result of all this labor, however, consisted of no more than a three page letter and an "Attached Note" of less than five pages. That in this way the mountain brought forth such a tiny mouse may be due to the fact that, in view of the great attention give to the Schillebeeckx case in the press, the authorities in Rome would have preferred to let it just fizzle out without issuing any real verdict. But such an action seemed hardly possible anymore, while an official acquittal would have meant a considerable loss of face for the Congregation. The short conclusion, therefore, appears to be the best solution of this dilemma that the Congregation could think up.

A considerable part of the letter is a detailed report of the steps taken so far and of Schillebeeckx' reactions. At first it seems a little odd that this information is presented so extensively to the defendant, who must be only too well aware of it all. Apparently, however, the letter was meant for other readers as well: the Cardinals who "examined" the various documents, the Pope who approved the "conclusions." And, of course, its genre really is that of the summing up of a judge. When at the end of the factual report of the case one reads the phrase "Consequently, speaking in their name and as Prefect of this Congregation, I wish to communicate the following to you," one almost sees Cardinal Seper rising to his feet behind the bench and looking at the accused standing before him, the press closing in on both of them.

What follows is rather an anticlimax. One hears that the investigation has resulted in clarifications and corrections, which Schillebeeckx is asked to make known to his readers, and that some ambiguities remain, which he is urged to review "in the light of Catholic teaching." His willingness to do so should be "attested publicly." For details one is referred to the "Attached Note," but expectations as to what this might contain are rather dampened beforehand by a disconcerting restriction. The letter states that there has not been time (!) to go into two of the most fundamental points: Schillebeeckx' view on the relations between Revelation and experience, and his theological procedure, which the Congregation calls a "*manuductio* of an apologetic kind." Therefore, no conclusions on these two points. For the moment Schillebeeckx is given no more than a pointer to an earlier document of the Congregation, directed against Küng, and a tautological reminder of "the need of a complete conformity to the principles which all theological work ought to follow."

The Note is a rather perplexing product. It is said to be based "essentially" on the report of the colloquy in Rome and on Schillebeeckx' written Response of 1977. There are frequent references to these two documents, various parts of which are literally quoted. This would seem to be a device mainly for Schillebeeckx' benefit. Somehow one cannot quite see busy Cardinals, let alone the Pope, turning the pages of the earlier documents to check statements, even if the texts were available to them. Or was the Note meant to be published on its own—as, eventually, it was—and were the references included as (hardly verifiable) proof of the Congregation's fairness to the defendant? That all the documents were going to be published so that even "outsiders" could compare the results, as happened only a few weeks after the Congregation dispatched its conclusions, must have been beyond Roman expectations.

Now, however, even a superficial check can make clear that the Congregation made a revealing selection of "results" from the documents. Not a few of the literal quotations turn out to be taken from its own contributions to the "conversation" in Rome, even when they start with a phrase like "Schillebeeckx 'grants' " (I, A/1), suggesting that he himself is quoted later on as well. Moreover, his replies are mostly cut short before he starts adding qualifications, for instance on the need of hermeneutical understanding. One also finds disquieting innuendos (that Schillebeeckx "no longer dodges" the explicit acknowledgment of Jesus' divinity, and now "acknowledges" his pre-existence: I, A/2) and "refinements" that are in fact literal quotations from Schillebeeckx' book (I, B/2; during the colloquy Schillebeeckx just pointed out the right page where his statement could be found). In several places the Congregation's summary of Schillebeeckx' viewpoint is elliptic, to say the least.[1] In expressions like "the terms used by the Church" the word "Church" clearly has a restrictive sense, as equivalent for "teaching office of the Church," or even for the Congregation itself. Formulas of faith are once more called "permanently true," though in his reply Schillebeeckx had indicated that the qualification "permanently" was superfluous and misleading (I, A/2; cf. doc. IV, A d/3). And, of course, the list is a very odd mixture of statements, arranged under purely formal headings, namely insofar as they were considered to be just clarifying, adding nuances to or even correcting earlier assertions. In the latter section, at first sight the more important one, the Congregation has thought it necessary to include expressions which Schillebeeckx has agreed to be "a little too apodictic," "unfortunate" or "not enough." One finds a curious mixture of theological and historical points, of fundamental and very peripheral items, of bald statements and involved, sophisticated arguments. Worst of all: the context of the statements, which according to the accepted standards of present day theology is vital to their understanding, is usually left out. In this sense the Note has returned to the earlier Roman practice of judging loose sentences, cut off from qualifications and context. What remains is basically a "list of errors."

Even more revealing is the second section of the Note, said to contain "persisting ambiguities" which Schillebeeckx is urged to "review in the light of the Catholic faith." These are four in number and concern such widely diverging topics as the grounds for Schillebeeckx' faith in the virginal conception of Jesus, the binding force of the "faith of the Church" (meant, of course, is: of its teaching office) for theology, the relations between Jesus' resurrection and his appearances and Schillebeeckx' rejection of the term "anhypostasis." Most of these points had already been covered in the earlier section, which further complicates the tracking down of "ambiguities," let alone their removal. The second "ambiguity," on theological methodology, is obviously connected very directly with the two fundamental issues that the accompanying letter expressly leaves out of its conclusions. Is the request to reconsider this question, then, to be the starting point of a further discussion?[2] The curious ambiguity of the Note can best be illustrated, however, by the third topic, on Jesus' resurrection and appearances. The discussion of this item during the colloquy in Rome is said to have been "not entirely satisfactory," both with regard to an historical reconstruction (which the Congregation now acknowledges to be "less relevant" to their investigation) and to "assertions which are central to the subject." Having remarked that Schillebeeckx' reply did not answer the difficulty on this point, a restatement is asked for, after which the Note refers to a passage from Schillebeeckx' "response" of 1977, already quoted in the Note and considered to be an important correction. One wonders if the author of the Note himself is clear as to what Schillebeeckx should do next.

At the end of his letter Cardinal Seper invited Schillebeeckx to propose a practical way to publish both the "clarifications" and his restatements of the "ambiguities." He suggests that Schillebeeckx write an article on the basis of the Note, which should be prepared "in agreement" with the Congregation. Just in time, however, he appears to have realized that this was really asking too much. He is "ready to consider any other method [Schillebeeckx] might propose." That his request, at least as far as the "clarifications" were concerned, was going to be granted by a publication of all the documents, and therefore also of the "concessions" the Congregation had so painstakingly collected but now in their proper context, must have been something of a surprise.

THE LETTER

V. Letter of Cardinal Franjo Seper,
Prefect of the Congregation for the Doctrine
of the Faith,
to Reverend Father Edward Schillebeeckx, O.P.,
(November 20, 1980)

Reverend Father,

For some time now our Congregation has been in touch with you for the purpose of gaining clarification on the Christological positions you have taken in your book *Jesus: An Experiment in Christology.*

As far back as October 20, 1976, after finding that the book contained ambiguous statements which could be a source of danger to your readers, the Congregation, via Cardinal Willebrands whom it kept informed of the ongoing investigation, addressed to you a list of questions on the content of your book and the method used in it.

On April 13, 1977 you answered these questions in a letter which offered various explanations; these did not remove all the difficulties as was explained to you in an "Evaluation of the Answers" which our Congregation sent to you on July 6, 1978.

Meanwhile you had published *Gerechtigheid en liefde: Genade en bevrijding* (1977; ET: *Christ: The Experience of Jesus as Lord,* 1980), the second volume of the trilogy on Christology which you had announced. A few months later you sent to the Congregation your little book *Tussentijds verhaal over twee Jezusboeken* (1978; ET: *Interim Report on the Books Jesus and Christ,* 1981), together with a card saying: "In this little book I have explained passages which are somewhat unclear or are the subject of debate in my books on Jesus Christ."

A careful study of this last-named publication reveals that it contains many interesting clarifications but also that your own position on fundamental points of the Catholic faith remains ambiguous. Consequently, given the seriousness of the questions under examination, the Congregation for the Doctrine of the Faith decided to invite you to a conversation in which these matters would be discussed, in keeping with articles 13–15 of its procedural regulations (*Ratio agendi*). Through Cardinal Willebrands you were asked on July 6, 1978 to be kind enough to come to Rome in order to clarify your position on Christology through a discussion with some delegates of our Congregation. The same letter also informed you of the essential points to be taken up in the conversation.

After further contacts, which were delayed by, among other things, the deaths in succession of Popes Paul VI and John Paul I, Cardinal Willebrands informed the Congregation (in a letter of June 30, 1979) that you had agreed to take part in the conversation. As a result, after the correspondence needed in order to settle the time and circumstances of the conversation, the meeting was finally held on December 13, 14 and 15, 1979 in the offices of the Congregation. The other participants were Msgr. A. Bovone, who chaired the conversations, Msgr. A. Descamps, and Fathers A. Patfoort, O.P. and J. Galot, S.J.

At a meeting with the authorities of the Congregation which immediately preceded the colloquium you were reminded that the purpose of the latter was not to proceed to a judgment or make decisions but to supply the further information needed on your Christological position. It was said, finally, that at the end of the conversation a report of it would be drawn up which, once accepted by the two parties, would be examined by the member Cardinals of the Congregation for the Doctrine of the Faith.

Assembled in a regular meeting, the Cardinals undertook this examination in the light of the explanations given in your written answer of April 17, 1977, and in the conversation of December 13–15, 1979.

The Cardinals found that the procedure followed had proved useful since it enabled you to offer explanations regarding the purpose, method and literary genre of your writings and to clear up a number of ambiguities.

In formulating their conclusions, which have been approved by the Holy Father, the Cardinals emphasized the fact that these conclusions held only for the three works named at the beginning of this letter.

Consequently, speaking in their name and as Prefect of this Congregation, I wish to communicate the following to you:

1. The Congregation notes the clarifications, refinements and corrections concerning your published works which you made at the conversation and in your letter (cf. the appended document, pp. 1–4).

2. It judges, however, that on certain points the explanations given are not enough to remove ambiguities (cf. the appended document, pp. 4–5).

For this reason, I ask you:

(1) To make known to the public which has access to your works the clarifications, refinements and corrections which emerge from the explanations recently given to the Congregation. Account must be taken of the fact that the book *Jesus* is now known to a wide readership. For this reason, your explanations, which on decisive points go further than the statements made in the published books, are important not only to the ecclesiastical magisterium but also to your readers who have a right to have such significant information made available to them.

(2) To review in the light of Catholic teaching the points on which there is still some ambiguity, and to attest publicly your willingness to act in accordance with this request.

Furthermore it must be recognized that despite the breadth of its program the conversation was unable to go deeply enough into the clarifications required on the one hand by your view of the relations between Revelation and experience and, on the other, by the role you assign in theology to a *manuductio* of an apologetic kind. For this reason and because of the doubts that still remain, the Congregation, though abstaining for the time being from passing a judgment on this subject, cannot but emphasize the need of a complete conformity to the principles which all theological work ought to follow. With regard to the connection between Revelation and experience (and the consequences of this relationship for the normative role of the *formal* teachings of the Bible and magisterial documents), the Congregation calls your attention especially to what it has said in the Declaration *Mysterium Ecclesiae*, 5 (*AAS* 65 [1973] 402–4).

I would be grateful, Reverend Father, if you would let me know what you consider to be the most effective way of meeting the requests I have stated. The Congregation, for its part, thinks of an article which you would write in agreement with it and in which you would take as your guide the document appended to this letter. But it is ready to consider any other method you might propose.

We are sending a copy of this letter to His Eminence Cardinal J. Willebrands who as Grand Chancellor of the University of Nijmegen is keeping au courant with this matter, and another to the Very Reverend Master General of the Order of Friars Preachers, your Ordinary.

Awaiting a favorable answer from you, I beg you, Reverend Father, to be assured of my respect and devotion.

[signed] *Franjo Cardinal Seper*
Prefect

Attached Note

This note is intended to explain in greater detail the general statements by the Congregation that are made in the accompanying letter. The points made in it are based essentially on the report of the conversation of December 13–15, 1979 (*Conversation*) and on the written response made by Fr. Schillebeeckx, April 13, 1977, to the questions which the Congregation had asked of him, likewise in writing (*Letter*).

I. Clarifications, refinements and corrections made by Professor
    Schillebeeckx
    A. Clarifications of a dogmatic kind

Preliminary note. The author does not intend to offer a complete Christology, but seeks rather to use the results of historico-critical exegesis in order to bring closer to the person of Jesus those who live on the periphery of the Church and the faith. His work is intended as a *manuductio,* as a work of apologetics in a sense or of fundamental theology (*Conversation,* 4 [= 165]).

(1) Professor Schillebeeckx "grants" that "when a theologian applies himself to an historical or exegetical investigation, he cannot sincerely regard himself as having to leave aside *the affirmations of faith that have been made by the Catholic Church*" and, in particular, "what has been defined by the ecumenical councils and in infallible papal statements," and that "in the judgments he really makes about things as they are a [dogmatic] theologian must adopt as the supreme norm of his thinking not his own conception of the Jesus of history but the thought of the Church about Jesus" (*Conversation,* 4–5 [165–66]). Consequently, every interpretation must be concerned to be a faithful and homogeneous translation of the formulas of faith which are "permanently true" (*Conversation,* 3 [162]).

(2) Unlike his approach in his books and in particular in the epilogue of *Interim Report,* he no longer dodges the explicit acknowledgment of the divinity of Jesus in the very terms used by the Church (*Conversation,* 5, end, and 6, end [167 and 168]). He acknowledges the pre-existence of the divine Person of the Son (*Conversation,* 6 [168]; *Letter,* 5, par. 2, line 4 from the end [64]) and a "hypostatic identification" of the Son of God with the "mode of being personally human" of Jesus.

(3) He states that in his view the relation of *Jesus* to the Father implies the *consciousness of being the only Son,* and this even if Jesus himself never used the term "the Son" (*Conversation,* 10 [174]), and that the explicit identification between the Kingdom and Jesus is a legitimate explicitation of Jesus' self-awareness, and that this is perceptible in the ancient Q tradition (*Letter,* 16 [82–83]).

(4) He states that "in virtue of the magisterium of the Church which has spoken on this point" he believes in the *virginal birth of Jesus* (*Conversation,* 14 [179]).

(5) He acknowledges that "*the sacrifice of Jesus expiates* our sins" (*Conversation,* 8 [171]).

(6) He states that "as far as [he] is concerned, it is clear that Jesus intended to found the Church" (choice of the Twelve as representatives of the twelve tribes of Israel; *Conversation,* 11 [175]).

B. Refinements on the import of some formulas and arguments

(1) With regard to the mystery of the Incarnation:

—The expression: "hypostatic identification" of the Word and the humanity of Jesus, an expression which the author says he prefers to the expression "hypostatic union" (*Jesus,* 667), does not in his mind exclude the reality of the hypostatic union (*Conversation,* 7 [168]: "I accept the hypostatic union"); the author is convinced that his formula captures the true substance of the hypostatic union (*Letter,* 14 [78]: "In my judgment, this restates the traditional hypostatic union in its purest form") and that he is in agreement with Chalcedon when it speaks of *unus et idem* ("one and the same") who is at once true God and true man.

—The expression "personally human mode of being" or "personalist humanity" or again the statement that "Jesus is 'humanly a person' " does not mean for him that the man Jesus has a human person (*Conversation,* 7 [168]); such expressions are meant only to emphasize the human fullness of Jesus as *verus homo,* "true man" (*Conversation,* 7 [168]). As a dogmatic theologian he never says that Jesus is a human person (*Conversation,* 6 [168]; n.b. this is put much better in *Letter,* 13 [77–78], etc.).

(2) With regard to the institution of the Eucharist, he adds that "the texts of institution [of the Eucharist] as we now find them [in the] liturgical formulas" are "an historical anamnesis of what happened at the Last Supper," and that "the origin of these [sacramental] words and of the Eucharist in its entirety is to be found in the Last Supper and in what Jesus said and did at the Last Supper" (*Conversation,* 12 [176]).

C. Corrections and restatements by the author

The author states that he came to see the following corrections as necessary, partly as a result of continued study, partly because he became aware that some of his concepts were "unfortunate" and could be misunderstood.

These corrections and restatements have to do with the following points and propositions:

(1) "The honorific title[s] 'Son of God' and 'the Son' . . . were *Christian* identifications of Jesus of Nazareth [made] after his death. Jesus never spoke of himself as 'the Son' or 'Son of God'; there is no passage in the Synoptics pointing in that direction [i.e., in the view of critical scholarship]" (*Jesus,* 258).

—*Correction:* "The passage quoted is a little too apodictic. I have softened it in *Christ*" (*Conversation,* 10 [173–74]).

(2) In Mark 14:25 (the account of eucharistic institution) "we see the effect of the Church's activity subsequent to Easter," and specifically in the second half of the verse: "until that day when I drink it new in the Kingdom of God" (*Jesus,* 308).

—*Correction:* "This way of putting it is unfortunate. . . . What is secondary is the combining of the two parts of the *logion.* I consider both parts to be in fact *ipsissima verba.* I have developed this point further in *Interim Report*" (*Conversation,* 12–13 [176–77]).

(3) "In *Jesus* [346–47] I did not make enough of a connection between the empty tomb and the resurrection. I realized subsequently that for the authors of the New Testament the link was a closer one than I had thought at first. In this sense, the discovery

of the empty tomb is perhaps a sign that mediates faith." "On this point my thought has progressed between *Jesus* and *Interim Report*" (*Conversation*, 15 [167]).

(4) "The 'Q community' does not know of appearances."

—*Correction:* "In any case, this is the most hypothetical part of my entire book. Although I regard the hypothesis of the "Q community" as a serious one, I am not unaware of the doubts that exist concerning it. My intention is simply to say that the faith of the community in the resurrection is not based solely on the sign of the empty tomb and the appearances" (*Conversation*, 16 [180].

(5) Even though what the author says about the appearances in the *Conversation* is not entirely satisfying (cf. below, II, 3), we do on occasion find in the *Letter* (17 [86]) a refinement and at the same time a correction that is of some importance. In interpreting the origin of the statements about the appearances Fr. Schillebeeckx uses the concept of *metanoia* (conversion). This approach risks not paying adequate attention to the qualitative difference between the appearances with which Jesus blessed his disciples and a "conversion experience" as such. In this context the following statement is important: "Perhaps my use of the word 'conversion' both in a moral and, above all, in a Christological sense is confusing. In any case, when I use this terminology of conversion the essential element in it is the Christophany, just as it is in the terminology of the appearances: *ōpthē* ('he was seen'). It is the living Christ, the risen One, who opens their eyes."

II. Limits of the end-results, and persisting ambiguities

(1) The answer given to the question about the virginal conception of Jesus Christ is formally correct but seems very limited in its value and scope when the author says: "I believe it in virtue of the magisteriuim" (*Conversation*, 14 [179]).

(2) On certain important points (cf. above, p. 1 of this Note) the author grants that the faith of the Church binds him as a dogmatic theologian or binds dogmatic theology. But quite often the statements made in his books give the impression that this binding force is limited to the dogmatic theologian in the narrow sense of the term. However, in fact the foundation provided by faith is valid for all the disciplines of Catholic theology, even if these make use of partially different methods.

(3) The statements made in the conversation with regard to

the relation between resurrection and appearances are not entirely satisfactory (*Conversation,* 16–18 [181–84]). This observation applies not only to hypotheses used in explaining the historical origin of the Easter faith (*Conversation,* 16 [181–82]) but also—and this is more relevant to a judgment to be passed by the Congregation for the Doctrine of the Faith—to various assertions which are central to the subject, as, for example: "The appearances as such are not the formal basis of our faith in the resurrection" (*Conversation,* 16 [182]). Such a statement does not answer the difficulty raised in the conversation, and therefore the ambiguity persists. (Cf., however, the passage from *Letter* that was cited above [I, C, 5]).

(4) The systematic and repeated rejection of the word *anhypostasis* (cf. *Jesus,* 656, bottom; 661, last line; 664, line 15ff; 667, line 2ff; *Conversation,* 7 [168]: "I prefer to avoid the anhypostasis implied in neo-Chalcedonianism") will be an abiding source of ambiguities. As we know, the author means thereby to "deny only that there was any human lack in the humanity of Jesus" (*Letter,* 13 [62]), but the word *hypostasis* is not the word *person* and its meaning for our contemporaries is not "spiritual nature" but "a reality that is distinct and independent in its existence." Consequently, the rejection of anhypostasis is not limited to a denial of any lack in the humanity of Jesus, but tends rather to make the reader see in this humanity a reality that is distinct and independent in its existence and to make him imagine that "inconceivable 'over against' between the man Jesus and the Son of God" which Schillebeeckx himself wishes to eliminate (*Jesus,* 667). The reader will find himself shuttling back and forth between two meanings: human person, not a human person.

[signed]   *Franjo Cardinal Seper*
Prefect

NOTES

1. For a careful and detailed analysis of the Note in relation to the earlier documents, cf. Herwi Rikhof, "Of Shadows and Substance: Analysis and Evaluation of the Documents in the Schillebeeckx Case," *Journal of Ecumenical Studies* 19 (1982) 244–267, a somewhat shortened version of the article

which later appeared in *Tijdschrift voor Theologie* 22(1982) 376–409 (here I quote from the American version). Rikhof first compares the documents in chronological order, after which he tries to track down the various points contained in the Note through the earlier documents. I am obviously indebted to this laborious but very necessary study for more details than can be acknowledged explicitly. A clear example of the unsatisfactory way in which Schillebeeckx' ideas are summarized can be found in Rikhof, *art. cit.*, 266 (on the Church, *Note* I, A/6).

   2. Cf. also the "Preliminary Note" in the Note (I, A), where the Congregation seems to consider the two sentences taken from the colloquy as a "clarification," even though it "abstains from passing a judgment" on this point (cf. the accompanying letter). Rikhof rightly points out that this is an impossible situation: once the Congregation had discovered the difference of method, it should explicitly have discussed it, "for the 'logical space' which determines the sense of the whole discussion is more or less called in question" (*art. cit.* 249, cf. 248–250). Schillebeeckx, on the other hand, should not have taken up the Congregation's distinction between dogmatics and apologetics, as it disguises the basic differences between him and the Congregation (*ibid.* 250–254).

EPILOGUE

At a press conference a few days after he had received Cardinal Seper's letter Schillebeeckx drew attention to one of its phrases, namely that for the Cardinals of the Congregation the procedure followed had proved useful because a number of ambiguities had been cleared up. He wondered whether this meant that his text had been cleared up and even corrected, or the (initial) interpretation of it by the Congregation. I think there can hardly be any doubt that the Roman authorities never implied that their ideas needed to be clarified. The only form of clarity they can recognize is: to be clearly in agreement with the Congregation's interpretation of the Christian faith, considered to be the only correct one, and "permanently true."

But the desire for "clarification" and "clear language" on which the Congregation repeatedly insists is in itself already quite characteristic. For the Congregation such "clarity" is a self-evident ideal in every form of theology; in its view the primary task of theology is to supply "doctrine" for the internal life and activity of the Church which can be recognized as such, a teaching geared to produce certainty and tranquillity. Modern theology has frequently exposed this ideal as—ironically enough—very much historically determined; it stems from the confessional controversies and from a philosophy that was under the spell of Descartes; it is geared more to a well-functioning government and an efficient administration of justice than to pastoral preaching or liturgical celebration. In the final analysis, the quest for clarity is in conflict with the specific character of religious, analogical language that draws its vitality precisely from the expressive, symbolical elements that human beings must use in approaching the mystery of God.[1] Cardinal Alfredo Ottaviani, the former Prefect of the Congregation, is said to have voiced this same difficulty in his own way, in a paradoxical statement that made the rounds and was attributed to him (the attribution was, of course, never confirmed, but the statement is compatible with Ottaviani's often manifested sense of self-mockery): It is just as well that the letters of Paul the Apostle were never submitted to us for approval; they would never have satisfied our strict requirements of clarity and unambiguousness.

At the press conference Schillebeeckx offered another suggestive comment. The four "persisting ambiguities" he was requested to clarify could really be reduced, he thought, to one question: What is in your interpretation the function of the Church's teaching authority in theology? This comment has since been amply documented in Rikhof's revealing analysis of the whole "investigation." He has shown that, first of all, Schillebeeckx' exposition on theological method and approach, which forms the most substantial part of his Response of 1977 and is vital for an understanding of all he has written, has not been taken up seriously. During the "conversation" in Rome only certain aspects of it were broached in the questions, while the final document, apart from some allusions and a "Preliminary Note" of strangely enigmatic character, contains only the declaration that the Congregation "abstains from passing a judgment" on this matter, as on the closely connected theme of Revelation and experience. Moreover, one can clearly recognize a shift of attention in the documents from the central issues (especially Incarnation) to elements which were less important, if not marginal, in Schillebeeckx' books (the virgin birth, the expiatory character of Jesus' sacrifice). Even more suggestive is the fact that the documents gradually move away from matters of theological methodology and content and concentrate more and more on authority and obedience.[2] Of course, the necessity of obedience had been implicit in the procedure from the beginning, but if one compares the quite meager harvest of "concessions" on the level of theological content in the Note with the first document, which had at least some standing as a theological inquiry, the narrowing of perspective is quite startling.

This emphasis on authority and obedience was amply born out in what followed after the final document. Schillebeeckx took some time before replying, and meanwhile rumors about his press conference, mistakenly reported in the *Informations Catholiques Internationales,* among others, and the publication of the earlier documents not quite unexpectedly caused some irritation at the Congregation. On February 19 Schillebeeckx sent the published documents and a recent article on Revelation and experience to the Congregation, with a letter which stated that in this way he considered to have published the "clarifications etc." as required. He also offered some suggestions for a publication on the "persisting ambiguities." About a month later the Congregation replied in rather a bad temper—there is, for instance, some sarcastic comment on the fact that the arrival of the final documents had become known to the press—and complained that Schillebeeckx had failed to publish the "Attached Note," which was now openly called the "doctrinal balance sheet" ("bilan doctrinal") of the whole procedure. Therefore he is given what amounts to an ultimatum: within a month (!) he should present the contents of the Note in an article, or else simply publish the Note itself. If he should fail to do so, the Congregation would feel obliged to publish the Note. Since this letter was sent via Cardinal Willebrands at Utrecht, who happened to be absent for some time, Schillebeeckx only received it in early May, just before starting a lecture tour in the United States. But he had no intention anyway of publishing the Note or even a paraphrase of it in an article, and on June 26, without further warning, the final letter and Note appeared on the front page of the *Osservatore Romano,* in the official French version.

After this maneuver it was quite some time before Schillebeeckx could bring himself to write to the Congregation. Very likely he, too, had by now come to the conclusion that there really was no excuse for ordering him about like a schoolboy.[3] On November 24, two days before Joseph Ratzinger succeeded Cardinal Seper as head of the Congregation, he explained to the latter why he had not published the Note himself: essentially it contained no new elements compared with the earlier documents, except an evaluation by the Congregation. If published out of its context—"without which it makes no sense"—and, especially, without Schillebeeckx' own evaluation, his readers would only be confused—a danger always very much on the Congregation's mind. As for what Schillebeeckx calls the four "minor points" on which his clarifications were still expected, he felt only obliged to deal with the fourth one, on "anhypostasis." The other points concerned either his motive for belief (in the virgin birth) or purely historical matters, both of which were clearly outside the Congregation's competence according to its own rules. As for the sneer on his "leaking" the Cardinal's letter to the press, he reminded the Congregation that he had never, even in Rome, been asked to keep matters secret. And had he not been required to publish the results anyway?

In a published reflection on the final documents one gets a hint of what might be Schillebeeckx' "clarification" in the matter of "anhypostasis." He remarks that apparently the Congregation intends to keep insisting on certain traditional terms—even non-conciliar terms, like this one[4]—irrespective of whether their meaning can still be understood. In Rome it is feared that otherwise "the reader will find himself shuttling back and forth between two meanings: [Jesus is a] human person, not a human person." Schillebeeckx probably cannot quite see such a fear as very important to his readers; and anyway he has said extensively in which sense he understands the man Jesus as a person, for instance during the colloquy in Rome, and apparently the Congregation has accepted this "clarification." Is the only complaint, then, that he prefers to avoid certain traditional terms because they require too much historical explanation?[5] Or is it, once more, only a matter of obedience? This was certainly the message of a later letter in which the Congregation, without referring to Schillebeeckx' argument, tersely requested him to make a statement on all four of the "persisting ambiguities."

In the course of 1980, when he was still waiting for the Congregation's conclusion on the colloquy in Rome, Schillebeeckx had made a number of articles on the ministry in the Church into a small book, knowing quite well that, even more than his Christological interpretation, his ideas on the ministry were likely to invite a new "investigation"—an expectation which seems to be coming true. Schillebeeckx is certainly not a person who enjoys conflict. But he is convinced that it is a theologian's responsibility to reflect on pressing problems of the Church and offer his conclusions, welcome or not. Just possibly, however, the Congregation might want to avoid the publicity of another "Schillebeeckx case." There is some evidence, anyway, that the Congregation has recognized that its procedure is an inadequate means to assure what most Christians, Schillebeeckx above all, consider a legitimate concern of the Church's teaching office: faithfulness to the Gospel. At a press conference in Rome on December 7, 1982 the new Prefect of the Congregation, Cardinal Ratzinger, who made himself a name as a theologian at several universities in Germany, announced certain changes in the doctrinal procedure, among them that in the future the defendant may be accompanied at ecclesiastical hearings by a canon lawyer to advise him.[6]

But the doubts about the current procedure concern a far more fundamental level. Schillebeeckx himself thinks that in practice the Congregation still has not recognized the teaching of Vatican II that the Gospel is committed to "the entire holy people united with their shepherds"[7] and feels obliged to carry the responsibility for its faithful (re)interpretation on its own, inspired by a type of fundamental theology which has largely been abandoned. In the light of Vatican II, and even of the recent Roman document *Sapientia Christiana*, it is really inexcusable that a fact such as implied in the following statement seems to have carried no weight with the Congregation, or rather, does not appear to have even been considered: "The Society of Catholic Theologians in The Netherlands has devoted several of its sessions to this book [Schillebeeckx' *Jesus*] and discussed it extensively with the author. The numerous members who took part in the discussion saw no reason at all to question the orthodoxy of this theology. On the contrary, the Society came to the conclusion that this book should be recognized as an exemplary attempt to reflect on the Catholic faith in Jesus Christ and to justify it convincingly in the face of present-day critical thought."[8]

Another witness in Schillebeeckx' defense calls herself an "uneducated" person, one of the hundreds—among them a seventy-six-year-old farmer from Belgium, a girl of fourteen from Holland, a boy, also fourteen, from Ireland, a "servant" in a monastery, a prisoner in the Federal Correctional Institution at Seagoville, Texas—who have written personal letters in support of Schillebeeckx. A woman from a small town in Holland, Nijverdal, wrote to him in November 1979: "Many people like us, without any training (let alone theological training!) [have] nonetheless been brought into contact with your work through hard-working pastors who have been moved by it. There are many priests who have 'translated' your book on Jesus into useful lessons for our everyday lives. We have learned to think more expansively and freely than before. No tribunal, no scholar, no Pope can take that from us. The present Pope does not seem to believe in us, the common faithful. The worst thing he did to us while in Mexico was not his quite unrealistic way of talking about—of course—sexuality. The worst thing was that he wanted to subject the theologians to the bishops' control in order to bring the common faithful (such as my family) once more on firm ground! As if we would ever again want this! (. . .) Why did I, though uneducated, want to write this to you? Because, whatever may happen to you in Rome, your work goes on! In us! The believer in the street, the factory, the shop, and behind the counter in the kitchen! And in our children. These are the ones you have worked for! These are the ones you are suffering for!"

In lonely moments during the years of frustrating inquiries and priggish innuendos it must have been some comfort to receive this kind of support.

NOTES

1. During the colloquy in Rome Schillebeeckx had, once again, tried to call attention to the dangers of too great a theoretical precision, which involves the risk of reducing and destroying the mystery. Cf., e.g., "I reject the adjective 'exact' because it seems to say that the mystery is 'captured' in abstract conceptual knowledge of it whereas in fact it is only 'sighted' through the concept" (Doc. IV, A, d/1; cf. the whole of c and d, pp. 161–162). Statements such as this were not considered "useful" enough to be included in the Note.

2. Cf. Rikhof, *art. cit.* (Doc. V, note 1), esp. pp. 247–248, 254, 266–267.

3. The Flemish theologian A.R. Van de Walle, reviewing the Dutch/ French edition of this book, confessed that before reading it he had thought it a right decision on the part of Schillebeeckx to go to Rome for the colloquy, even though he had doubts about the whole procedure. After he had actually read the text of the documents, he changed his view. He confessed he had been shocked by the tone used against a theologian of Schillebeeckx' standing, which reminded him of the "insufferable superiority of certain 'healthy' people over against handicapped persons" ("De zaak Schillebeeckx," *Tijdschrift voor Geestelijk Leven* 37 [1981] 318–320).

4. As Schillebeeckx clearly indicated in his response (Doc. II, II/a, pp. 77/8).

5. E. Schillebeeckx, "Theologische overpeinzing achteraf," *Tijdschrift voor Theologie* 20 (1980) 422–426, quot. 426; German tr.: "Theologische Reflexionen im Rückblick," *Theologie der Gegenwart* 24(1981) 142–146.

6. Reported, among others, in *The Tablet*, Vol. 236 (1982) 1276. The new rules are said to have been asked for by the West German and Swiss bishops; they would seem to be inspired, however, by the initiative of Bas van Iersel to be present at Schillebeeckx' "conversation" in Rome.

7. *Dei verbum*, II, No. 10. The Council explicitly rejected the traditional distinction between "regula proxima fidei" (teaching authority) and "regula remota" (Scripture and tradition). The Council further states: "This teaching office is not above the word of God, but serves it" (*ibid.*). Cf. Schillebeeckx, *art. cit.* (note 5), 424.

8. Published, along with several other statements, in *Archief van de kerken* 35 (1980) 669. Personal reactions to the Schillebeeckx case have been summarized in T.M. Schoof, "Getuigen in de 'zaak Schillebeeckx,'" *Tijdschrift voor Theologie* 20 (1980) 402–421 (summary in English).